Lectures on Regulatory and Competition Policy

Lectures on Regulatory and Competition Policy

IRWIN M. STELZER

The Institute of Economic Affairs

First published in Great Britain in 2001 by
The Institute of Economic Affairs
2 Lord North Street
Westminster
London sw1p 3lb
in association with Profile Books Ltd

A CIP catalogue record for this book is available from the British Library.

ISBN 0 255 36511 X

Many IEA publications are translated into languages other than English or are
reprinted. Permission to translate or to reprint should be sought from the
General Director at the address above.

Typeset in Stone by MacGuru
info@macguru.org.uk

Printed and bound in Great Britain by Hobbs the Printers

CONTENTS

THE AUTHOR

Irwin M. Stelzer is a senior fellow and director of the Hudson Institute's regulatory studies programme. Prior to joining the Hudson Institute in 1998, Stelzer was resident scholar and director of regulatory policy studies at the American Enterprise Institute. He also is the US economic and political columnist for the *Sunday Times* (London) and the *Courier Mail* (Australia), a contributing editor of the *Weekly Standard*, a member of the Publication Committee of *The Public Interest*, and a member of the board of the Regulatory Policy Institute (Oxford).

Stelzer founded National Economic Research Associates, Inc. (NERA) in 1961 and served as its president until a few years after its sale in 1983 to Marsh & McLennan. He has also served as managing director of the investment banking firm of Rothschild Inc. and director of the Energy and Environmental Policy Center at Harvard University.

As a consultant to several US and United Kingdom industries with a variety of commercial and policy problems, Stelzer advises on market strategy, pricing and antitrust issues, and regulatory matters.

His academic career includes teaching appointments at Cornell University, the University of Connecticut, and New York University, and an associate membership of Nuffield College, Oxford. He is a former member of the Litigation and Administrative Practice Faculty of the Practicing Law Institute. He served on the Massachusetts Institute of Technology Visiting Committee for the Department of Economics, and has been a teaching member of Columbia University's Continuing Legal Education Programs.

Stelzer received his Bachelor and Master of Arts degrees from New York University and his doctorate in economics from Cornell University. He has written and lectured on economic and policy developments in the United States and Britain, and written extensively on policy issues such as America's competitive position in the world economy, optimum regulatory policies, the consequences of European integration, and factors affecting and impeding economic growth. He has served as economics editor of the *Antitrust Bulletin* and is the author of *Selected Antitrust Cases: Landmark Decisions* and *The Antitrust Laws: A Primer*.

FOREWORD

For many years, Dr Irwin Stelzer has been a leading economic commentator, both in Britain and the United States. He is known to many because of his weekly column in the *Sunday Times*, and he has been very active as a lecturer in different parts of the world.

There is never any problem in attracting audiences to lectures given by Irwin. Not only are they based on sound and fundamental economic principles, but they are invariably delivered with such wit and good humour that even his opponents find it hard to disagree. In this Occasional Paper, some of Dr Stelzer's lectures – from the late 1980s to the recent past – are reprinted for the benefit of a wider audience than they have already reached. The lectures (some given to IEA audiences) cover three broad fields in which the author's views are widely respected – competition policy, regulation and policy towards the energy industries and the environment.

Dr Stelzer places himself firmly within the free market tradition in economics. When confronted with a problem, his instinct is to look for a market solution rather than advising the government to intervene. For him, regulation is a last resort: attempts to extend competition should always take priority. Moreover, he has a gift not all economists possess: he expresses his ideas in lucid, jargon-free English so they are comprehensible to anyone with an interest in economic issues, whether formally trained in economics or not. His essays are a pleasure to read.

Of course, 'free market economics' is a broad church. Some of those within that tradition will disagree with specific proposals made by Irwin. Some, particularly those of an Austrian persuasion, will not share his enthusiasm for competition policy; others will be more wary of the US regulatory regime than he is; others may be critical of his ideas for dealing with the Organisation of Petroleum Exporting Countries.

But whether one agrees with everything Irwin proposes is irrelevant. These essays leave three overwhelming impressions with the reader. The first is that the author provides a carefully considered, powerful and deeply felt exposition of the benefits of letting markets work; the second is that he exposes the fallacies which underly the 'market failure' tradition; the third is that, using economic principles and his own experience, he demonstrates the prevalence of government failure and the unintended consequences which flow from government action.

As in all Institute papers, the views are those of the author, not of the Institute (which has no corporate view), its Managing Trustees, Advisory Council members or senior staff. But the Institute is delighted to publish Dr Stelzer's provocative, good-humoured and stimulating insights into some of the most significant economic issues of the day.

COLIN ROBINSON

Editorial Director, Institute of Economic Affairs

Professor of Economics, University of Surrey

July 2001

To Cita who sat, uncomplaining, through these lectures

INTRODUCTION

I was delighted when the Institute of Economic Affairs decided that it might be of use to economists and students engaged in the difficult task of developing competition, regulatory and, more important, deregulatory policies to have these lectures available to them in handy form. In each of these talks I try to apply basic economic principles to the issues facing those charged with the responsibility for crafting general policies to promote competition (Part 1); to issues facing regulators (Part 2); and to the quagmire into which successive generations of legislators and pundits have fallen and continue to fall – energy policy (Part 3).

The recurring theme in these talks is that markets are a more efficient instrument for allocating resources than even the wisest of regulators or legislators. But for markets to function efficiently they must be effectively competitive. That is why – but not only why – the most important of all policies is competition policy, which must aim to root out barriers to competition among existing competitors, and practices that deter new entrants, functions that take on added importance in so-called 'high-tech industries', in which companies have a great incentive to erect shelters from the gale of creative destruction that is the key to better products and lower prices. Where competition is effective, the chore of deciding which businesses shall succeed and which shall fail, and how society's resources are deployed to satisfy consumer wants, can be left to Adam Smith's invisible hand.

Where competition is ineffective, the long arm of government comes into play. Its first goal should be to eliminate impediments to competition, to make on-going government intervention unnecessary. But there remain industries in which effective competition is not an immediately available alternative to the existing market structure. Such is the case at present in the so-called wires industries – in telephony, the 'last mile' of wire from the kerb into the home; in electricity, the transmission grids and distribution wires that connect consumers with the plants in which their power is generated.

I say 'at present' because if history teaches anything it is that many of the industries that we have considered to be 'natural monopolies' never were, or were at some point transformed by technology into industries in which effective competition is feasible. Such has been the case in the generation of electric power, where it was once thought that economies of scale were so extensive as to preclude more than a single seller from serving a market; in the production of natural gas, where concentrated control of large gas fields combined with lenders' insistence that pipeline projects be backed by 20 years of known reserves at one time made price regulation necessary; in the airline industry, where it was once believed that competition would lead to skimping on safety. New knowledge and new technology have combined to change our view, and we now have in both the UK and the US reasonably competitive generating and natural gas sectors, and a highly (although far from perfectly) competitive worldwide airline industry.

It is this process of constant change in industry structure and the possibility of competition which makes the economist's chore so interesting. He must resist the pleas of regulators and the companies that often exist cosily under the regulatory umbrella to retain embedded systems of price and other controls, while at the same time rejecting the arguments of those of his brethren who contend that all monopoly power is transitory, and that attempts to regulate it only delay the day when competition will emerge.

I contend in these talks that the presence of 'market failure' does not necessarily justify government intervention, and that 'government failure' is a danger lurking in any regulatory programme. But those facts, as powerful as they are in tipping us in the direction of preferring market forces to regulatory edicts, cannot obviate the need for consumer protection where market power is sufficient to permit exploitation in the form of inflated prices or degraded service. At times, as I point out in one of these lectures, consumer protection must come, not from the government, but from private sector lawyers acting on behalf of client-plaintiffs seeking awards of threefold the damages inflicted upon them, as American law prescribes. In order to reach decisions about the nature and extent of such injury, it is necessary to engage in the highly technical art of defining the markets in which real rivalry is occurring or may soon occur, a subject also covered in these talks.

The trick for the student of competition and regulatory policy, and one I hope these lectures will elucidate, is to include in any regulatory schemes that are deemed necessary to prevent monopoly exploitation such programmes as will foster competition, so that the eventual goal of the regulator can be to turn out the lights of his agency, and to go on to better things, as was the case with the Civil Aeronautics Board in the United States. After hard work by a group of academic economists fostered a legislative consensus that competition would serve consumers better than a system in which regulators determined which airlines might serve which markets at what prices, the regulators ceded the field to the market, with enormous benefits to consumers.

Another theme of these lectures is that men, and more recently women, matter. Just as great teachers can increase the probability that students will leave the lecture hall wiser than when they entered, and talented corporate executives can make a difference in the performance of an enterprise, so talented regulators can make a difference in the way any given set of rules is applied. In the hands of a knowledgeable economist, regulation based on 'cost' can come to mean marginal cost, a concept with real economic content, while in the hands of a less able person, perhaps one afflicted with an excessive devotion to accounting techniques, 'cost' can mean something quite different – and be useless as a guide to setting economically efficient prices. A regulator devoted to extending the scope of competition will hunt relentlessly for ways to encourage new entrants; another less visionary regulator might see his job to be the preservation of the viability of the monopoly service provider. Our two nations may be governments of laws, not men, but the way the laws are administered (and, indeed, drafted) by men will determine the balance drawn between regulation and competition as protectors of consumer interests.

A word about the form of these lectures. I have taken the liberty of lightly editing them to eliminate grammatical errors that crept in here and there, to delete what in retrospect seem to me to have been irrelevant asides or examples that are no longer pertinent, and to clarify some of the semi-technical terms that carelessly allowed to creep into these talks. I have also deleted the declarations of interest with which it is my custom to precede each presentation, warning the audiences of my relevant consulting relationships. Let me state them here: I have over the years consulted with numerous firms in a variety of industries in antitrust and regulatory matters.

I have not attempted to eliminate the duplications that appear in some of these lectures, as I am assuming that they will not be read in a single sitting. But I have added a few footnotes to reflect important events that have occurred since the preparation of these talks (indicated by asterisks). And I have retained the footnotes that appeared in my original talking notes (indicated by superior figures). It might strike the reader as strange that my lecture notes contain these footnotes. After all, one can hardly read footnotes to an audience. I include such notes in the texts from which I speak because the audiences on which these talks have been inflicted are typically very, shall we say, inquisitive, and I find it a comfort to have supporting authorities and data handy for the robust discussions that typically follow my talks.

The vigour of these discussions is, I think, due to the fact that the positions I take seem to satisfy no one. Those who oppose regulation in all circumstances, and who view all market power as transitory and more likely to be preserved than contained by regulation, find my willingness to abide regulatory regimes in certain circumstances unsettling. Which may be why none of these talks has been delivered on the campus of the University of Chicago! Indeed, it is a testimonial to the ecumenism of my IEA colleague Professor Colin Robinson that I am permitted to utter words in support of regulation in the hallowed hall of the Institute of Economic Affairs, and to the geniality of some of my associates at the Hudson Institute that they still find me an acceptable colleague.

Others find my bias against government intervention equally disturbing. There are a great many able and honourable men and women who sincerely believe that they can protect consumers better than can an unregulated marketplace. They see market imperfections under every bed, and do not believe that imperfectly but nevertheless effectively competitive markets can do a good job of balancing the interests of consumers, producers and investors. So they find my notion that we should call on their talents only in extreme circumstances, and my frequent critiques of the manner in which they exercise their vast powers, more than a little annoying. It is a tribute to their willingness to listen to my tales of regulatory horrors that we remain in close and interesting contact, an association that unnerves some of my colleagues in what are called conservative circles in Washington, DC, and in Britain.

Adding to their discomfort and to that of my many friends and clients in the business community is my support for stringent penalties for violation of competition laws, set forth most completely in a lecture delivered under the auspices of the Adam Smith Institute at the request of the Chancellor of the Exchequer. In the view of some of my critics, the imposition of jail terms on price fixers treats the business executives who engage in such practices as equivalent to the fraudster or common crook. Since price fixers are illicitly lightening the pockets of consumers every bit as much as any highwayman ever did, I see no distinction, except perhaps in the stringency of security required in the prisons to which they may be sent. My British colleagues tell me that their country is not 'culturally ready' for such penalties, while my American colleagues in the antitrust community assure me that only such criminal penalties can constrain the temptation of rivals to connive together for their mutual betterment, at high cost to consumers. In this instance, I side with my American friends.

Stirring up a bit of opposition from thoughtful colleagues, I must confess, is one of the goals of these lectures. After all, several of these talks were delivered to sleepy audiences at breakfast seminars, others to dozing scholars, businessmen and politicians after the ample lunches provided by the IEA as an inducement to attend its 'working lunch' series. The most intensely interested students of the subjects I cover do not seem to find a bit of scratchy stimulation out of place in those circumstances, judging by their lively response to my provocations. Such discussions, I believe, fulfil the purpose of the think tank that sponsors this little volume, and the one with which I am now affiliated: they make us think – me, as well as the audience.

It is my hope that the wider distribution of these lectures made possible by their publication will further one of the goals of both the Institute of Economic Affairs and the Hudson Institute – to show that a sensible application of the tools of the economist can maximise human freedom by demonstrating the desirability of steadily increasing the role of markets, and diminishing the areas of the economy controlled by regulators.

These remarks are the result of many wonderful advantages I have had over the years. The Hudson Institute has given me the freedom to muse on these topics, without any accompanying administrative burdens. The Institute of Economic Affairs has generously allowed me to participate in its stimulating seminars and meetings, and provided a UK platform for my talks. And many people have been generous with their wisdom: my late colleague Herman Roseman subjected me to his special form of scepticism about fashionable 'truths'; William Hogan, a professor at Harvard's Kennedy School of Government, taught me what should have been obvious but was not – that the prerequisite to a sensible answer is asking the right question; Alfred Kahn, now retired from Cornell University but still a leader in regulatory and antitrust economics, and John Shenefield, formerly head of the Antitrust Justice division and now in private practice, have patiently shared with me their knowledge of regulation and competition policy, respectively; and Gertrude Himmelfarb and Irving Kristol, historian and philosopher-king, respectively, have reminded me that economic efficiency ought not be the sole goal of public policy, and that man does not live by GDP alone.

Indeed, that point is one that must be kept in mind in all debates about competition policy. As John Shenefield and I have pointed out, competition policy has laudable social and political, as well as economic, purposes. Effective competition policy contributes to the diffusion of economic power and the maximisation of opportunities for all.[1] The removal of artificial impediments to entry is one of the prerequisites to a society that allows new, unrich entrepreneurs to pursue ideas that threaten the economic wellbeing of those who are astride an industry. Competition is the deadly enemy of class rigidity, a fact to which Great Britain is now awakening, thanks in good part to its Chancellor, Gordon Brown.

I would be remiss were I not also to thank Leyre Gonzalez, my assistant, who has laboured to put these lectures into proper order for publication.

Finally, these lectures owe much to my wife, Cita, who has helped with the research that underpins them, and whose grim fate it has been to read early drafts and insist that obscure passages be clarified, and then to sit dutifully through many of these talks.

---

1   *The Antitrust Laws: A Primer*, AEI Press, Washington, DC, 1998, pp. 10–12.

1 THOUGHTS ON COMPETITION POLICY

Procedures for private antitrust enforcement in the United States

This lecture was delivered at the Second Oxford Antitrust Law Conference at Queen's College on 12 September 1983 at a time when the notion that private parties might be permitted to sue to recover damages inflicted on them by dominant firms using anti-competitive tactics was, to put it mildly, anathema to the British bar and the business establishment. In it I attempted to explain that competition policy has a social objective, described in the introduction, above, and that sole reliance on government to enforce the laws is not as effective as is enlisting the aid of thousands of 'private attorneys-general' and their fee-seeking lawyers. British and European attitudes towards competition at the time of this talk should be compared with what I would term the more enlightened views that had evolved by the time of the last lecture in this section.*

This is a particularly good time to consider the basis and efficacy of private antitrust treble-damage actions, for just as the European Community has begun to give serious thought to the

---

*   Howard Kitt, a colleague at the time this lecture was prepared, made an enormous contribution to the research and writing.

advantages of such actions,[1] antitrust enforcement officials in the United States have begun to voice serious reservations about them.[2] I propose, today, to review the reasons private parties were granted what Senator Sherman described as 'some remedy in a court of general jurisdiction in the United States to sue for and recover the damages they have suffered'.[3] Then I would like to review the relative importance of such private actions in achieving the goals of US antitrust policy. Third, I would like to discuss the question of how the magnitude[4] of damages inflicted by antitrust violators can be measured. Fourth, I will attempt to appraise the defects and advantages of current US policy. Finally, I shall consider the applicability of the US experience to European competition policy.

The basis for US policy

Section 7 of the original Sherman Act – now Section 4 of the Clayton Act, as modified – created a private right of action not present under common law: any person 'injured in his business or property' by a violation of the Act could recover treble the damages inflicted on him, plus reasonable attorney's fees. As with other

---

1   See statement of William Hopper, MEP, and Thomas Sharpe, of the Institute for Fiscal Studies and our firm [at the time of this talk, National Economic Research Associates], as reported by Rebecca Smellie in 'The Competition Policy of the European Community: a Conference Report', *Government and Opposition*, vol. 18, no. 3, summer 1983, pp. 274, 282.

2   At the urging of William F. Baxter, Assistant Attorney-General in charge of the Antitrust Division, the Administration introduced a bill, entitled the 'National Productivity and Innovation Act of 1983'. See Note 55 below.

3   21 Congressional Record 2556 (1890).

4   Clayton Act, ch. 323, section 4, 38 Stat. 730, 731–2 (1914) (current version at 14 USC, section 18 [1976]).

provisions of our antitrust statutes, this section was rooted in concepts of both equity and economics.

One of the notions of equity that impelled Congress to adopt the treble-damage provision was revealed clearly in Senator Sherman's remarks during the Senate debate on his bill. He referred to the situation in which 'a humble man starts a business in opposition to them [the trusts], solitary and alone' and is forced out of business by a monopolist's predatory acts.

> Why, sir, I know of one case where a man in good
> circumstances, a thrifty, strong, healthy American was . . .
> met in just the way I have mentioned. If he had had the right
> to sue this company in the courts of the United States under
> this section he would have been able to indemnify himself
> for the losses that he suffered.[5]

So we have here the idea that the 'little fellow' should have an opportunity to recover from the 'big bully' any losses inflicted by the latter's illegal activity. Additionally, equity seemed to demand that something be done to equalise access to the courts: large corporations, with their bevies of lawyers, clearly had such access as a practical matter. But the small businessman did not. By providing the possibility that he might recover threefold damages and attorney's fees, the antitrust laws increased access to the judicial process by less well-heeled parties: 'This section opens the door of justice to every man, whenever he may be injured by those who violate the antitrust laws . . .'[6]

It is, of course, now fashionable for economists, particularly those of the Chicago School, to make light of these considerations, and to argue that antitrust policy has a purely economic objective:

---

5   See Note 2 above.
6   Congressman Webb of New York, 51 Congressional Record 9073 (1914).

to improve the efficiency with which resources are allocated.[7] I have elsewhere[8] argued the contrary, and will touch on that issue later, showing that a respectable body of opinion exists that supports the thesis that social goals – the preservation of numerous independent businesses; diffusion of economic power; a perception that the economic system is fair – are a valid basis for antitrust policy.[9]

But the treble-damage provision has economic goals as well. First, it changes the cost-benefit calculus of potential violators. The trebling of proved damages was and is designed to 'up the ante', to make violators know that they have a great deal to lose, if caught and assessed for damages. Of course, trebling is a crude punishment, not as precisely calibrated to fit and deter the crime as modern economists might prefer. But, as I shall discuss below, it seems to work. Some payment in excess of the mere return of ill-gotten gains is an important deterrent to illegal activities. Since the probability that the violation will be discovered at all is less than one, it would always pay to break the law if the penalty for doing so were merely the return of ill-gotten gains.

Second, trebling provides an incentive to bring suit – perhaps so great an incentive as to encourage the bringing of 'unfounded actions . . . in the hope that the cost of defending, plus the possible

---

7   See, for example, William H. Page, 'Antitrust Damages and Economic Efficiency: An Approach to Antitrust Injury', 7 U. Chi. L. Rev., 1980, pp. 472, 504.

8   Irwin M. Stelzer, 'Economic Defences in Antitrust Litigation', presented at European Study Conference on Economic Defences in Anti-Trust, London, 12 April 1983.

9   Hans B. Thorelli, *Federal Antitrust Policy: Origination of an American Tradition* (1955); Joel B. Dirlam and Alfred E. Kahn, *Fair Competition; the Law and Economics of Antitrust Policy* (1954); Stephen M. Axinn, 'Time to Rethink Antitrust Views', 5 The Nat'l L. J. 13, 1983.

penalty of having to pay treble damages and attorneys' fees, will bring about a settlement'.[10] Of that, more later.

Finally, the treble-damage and legal cost provisions give injured parties the *means* to pursue redress. If a plaintiff were certain of winning, single damages for him, plus incurred fees for his counsel, might be sufficient recompense to enable a small plaintiff to obtain counsel. But no such certainty exists. Hence, a plaintiff who cannot afford to finance a protracted antitrust suit must be in a position to promise his counsel something extra *if* the suit is successful – not only normal fees, but a portion of the punitive assessment.

To summarise: in addition to its social purposes, the provision for trebling damages has three economic bases: it raises the cost of violations; it provides injured parties with a strong incentive to pursue their grievances; it provides injured parties with the means with which to obtain representation.

The importance of private actions

The number of private actions brought under the antitrust laws has exceeded by ten times the number brought by the government since 1941.[11] Indeed, the number of private actions has exceeded the number of government-instituted proceedings since the early days of enforcement: between July 1890 and December 1903 some

---

10 E. Compton Timberlake, *Federal Treble Damage Antitrust Actions*, 1965, p. 13.
11 Senator Sherman's prediction that 'Very few actions will probably be brought ...' was wrong. Whether his further prediction was correct – 'but the cases that will be brought will be by men of spirit ...' – I leave to discussion by members of the defence and plaintiffs bar.

23 government cases and 34 private cases were brought.[12] The number of private suits brought does not, of course, necessarily reflect their relative importance in affecting business behaviour. And many private actions 'ride hard on the shoulders of a government criminal or civil case';[13] witness the numerous cases following government actions in the movie and electrical equipment industries. But the fact remains that private treble actions have clearly accomplished several purposes.

First, as Senator Sherman predicted, they have often permitted individual plaintiffs whose injury was too small to attract the resources of governmental enforcement authorities to seek and obtain redress. This ability has been augmented by resort to class actions, whereby individual plaintiffs with a common grievance pool their resources.

Second, the availability of this remedy has effectively supplemented the resources devoted to antitrust enforcement. As one Congressman stated during the debate on the Clayton Act, the right of private action was designed to take 'the business public into our confidence as allies of the Government in enforcing the antitrust laws ... '[14] It succeeded, as Phillip Areeda has pointed out: treble damages 'enlist private plaintiffs in the work of detecting, punishing, and thereby deterring wrongdoing'.[15]

---

12   Thorelli, op. cit., p. 597. Thorelli is 'convinced that the significance of these [early] cases, as a means of antitrust enforcement and as a proving ground for judicial opinion, was far greater than is customarily assumed'.

13   A. D. Neale and D. G. Goyder, *The Antitrust Laws of the United States of America: A Study of Competition Enforced by Law*, 1980, p. 415.

14   Congressman Floyd of Arkansas, 51 Congressional Record 16,319 (1914).

15   Phillip Areeda, 'Antitrust Violations without Damage Recoveries', 89 Harv. L. Rev. 1127 (1976). See also Phillip Areeda and Donald F. Turner, *Antitrust Law: An Analysis of Antitrust Principles and Their Application*, 1978, p. 227.

Third, private actions have not only been numerous, but effective deterrents to some business actions (critics would say to some competitive as well as anti-competitive activities). One critic of such actions and their consequences has pointed out that 'the private plaintiff had become the most important agent of enforcement'.[16] And my own experience has been that businessmen, especially when considering changes in marketing techniques, spend more time worrying about the possibility that competitors and dealers will file treble-damage actions than they do worrying about a Department of Justice (DOJ) initiated proceeding.[17] And this fear is well founded. As I pointed out earlier, the number of private actions far exceeds the number of government-instituted proceedings. These private actions are highly concentrated in the area of vertical relationships – relationships between dealers and their suppliers. My firm's study [at the time of this talk I was president of National Economic Research Associates] of 352 of the private antitrust cases filed in the Southern District of New York between 1973 and 1978,[18] undertaken for the Bar Association, revealed that almost three-quarters of those private actions alleged vertical price fixing and market allocation, exclusive dealing or tying requirements, or dealer terminations.[19]

16 Congressman Webb, op. cit., pp. 467, 468.

17 My own experience seems to parallel that of antitrust practitioners. 'There is no doubt that the possibility of treble damages is the aspect of American antitrust enforcement that is most feared by senior corporate management . . . [T]here can be little doubt that the spectre of treble damages does deter – the debate is over how much benefit is received for how much cost.' Joe Sims and Christopher L. Lawlor, 'Treble Damage Remedy Deserves Re-examination', *Legal Times of Washington*, 26 October 1981, p. 40.

18 This sample represents 58 per cent of all antitrust cases filed in those years.

19 'Statistical Analysis of Private Antitrust Litigation: Final Report', prepared by Joan Bodoff, National Economic Research Associates, Inc., for the American Bar Association Section of Antitrust Law (30 October 1979). For a convenient

So it seems clear that the disciplining effect of the antitrust statutes would be much diluted, particularly in the area of vertical arrangements, if sole reliance were placed on government actions. Private actions permit many businessmen to obtain a hearing in cases that are too small to attract DOJ action; or that rely on doctrines historically accepted by the courts but not in favour with the Reagan Administration enforcement officials;[20] or that hold out the prospect of profitable settlements.[21]

Businessmen and their sophisticated counsel know when some planned strategy is in that grey area between *per se* illegality and clear lawfulness. The fear of treble-damage actions by affected competitors makes them think twice, perhaps reshape the strategy to move it closer to the clearly unassailable category. Whether that threat also causes them to abandon some economically efficient and otherwise desirable business activities, as William Baxter has apparently concluded,[22] we will consider later.

Virtues and defects of US policy

At various points in this talk, I have already referred to some of the advantages of our policy decision to allow private parties to sue for recovery of threefold damages. Let me summarise those:

---

summary and discussion, see James P. Melican, Jr, 'The Treble Damage Case: Fact and Fiction', Antitrust L. J., vol. 49, issue 3, pp. 981–8, especially 984–6.

20 Note here Walton Hamilton's observation: 'A man knew when he was hurt better than an agency or government alone could tell him.' Walton Hamilton and Irene Till, *Antitrust in Action*, 1974, p. 10.

21 See Note 9 above.

22 See William F. Baxter, Presentation to the National Association of Manufacturers, 10 May 1983, especially pp. 5–6 (transcript).

1. The availability of this remedy to small businesses opens up the judicial system to those whose grievances are deemed too small to warrant government action.[23]

2. The treble-damage remedy, by providing an incentive to sue and the means for financing such antitrust suits, increases the resources devoted to enforcement.

3. The possibility of private actions makes the intensity and direction of antitrust enforcement less subject to the attitudes of the administration temporarily in control of the government's enforcement apparatus.

4. The threat of private actions clearly influences business behaviour, especially in the area of vertical relationships: '... It is perfectly clear that such actions do serve as a deterrent to violation of the statute ...';[24] and that the treble-damage action is 'a powerful and growing factor in the effectiveness of antitrust ...'[25]

The disadvantages of the availability of this remedy are claimed to be:

1. Nuisance suits are filed to obtain settlements that may be less costly to defendants than the litigation necessary to obtain vindication.[26]

2. Measurement of damages is virtually impossible. As one critic has put it, '... I challenge anyone to state with a straight face

---

23 This, of course, is closely tied to the class action, a topic too large for considera-
    tion here. See John G. Harkins, Jr, 'Another Look at Class Actions', 49 Antitrust L.
    J., 1981, p. 989.

24 Stelzer, op. cit.

25 Thorelli, op. cit., p. 418.

26 See Note 9 above.

that there is a single, objectively certain answer in cases of this sort as to what ill-gotten gains were pocketed or what damage was suffered, if any. With all due deference to those who wave the magic wand of expert testimony or sampling or other supposed sure-fire techniques for ascertaining damages ... those aids to resolution of the issue are uncertain at best, and outright deception at worst.'[27]

3.   Proliferation of suits that serve private, but not public, interests is encouraged.

4.   The threat of treble damages creates the possibility of a penalty unrelated in size to 'the anti-competitive effects of the conduct involved', and this overkill will create 'deterrents to efficient conduct'.[28] There are, in other words, 'Inefficient levels of deterrence'.[29]

5.   The treble-damage remedy, when applied to cases involving other than *per se* violations such as 'conduct that is clearly anti-competitive and is carried out in secret, as in the case of price fixing among competitors', is 'counterproductive'.

Because treble damages greatly increase the costs associated with the risk that some court might incorrectly condemn a particular procompetitive practice, the remedy can inhibit a wide variety of procompetitive arrangements. The remedy has a particularly pernicious effect on the incentives to innovate because it tends to overdeter licensing of intellectual property, an activity that usually increases efficiency and thereby increase[s] the returns to investments in R&D.[30]

---

27   Harkins, op. cit., pp. 996–7.
28   Congressman Webb, op. cit., pp. 472–6.
29   Ibid, p. 475.
30   William F. Baxter, 'Statement before the Committee on the Judiciary, US Senate, Concerning S. 737, S. 568 and S. 1383', 29 June 1983, p. 7 (mimeo).

That some of these criticisms are justifiable there can be little doubt. Lawyers, greedy for trebling and an award of attorney's fees, do bring antitrust actions (or attempt to convert ordinary contract disputes into antitrust actions) in the hope of receiving a settlement from defendants who find that course less costly than pursuing legitimate defences, or who seek to avoid unfavourable publicity.[31]

But this is a problem that can be solved without forgoing the advantages of private treble-damage actions. Courts can distinguish nuisance suits from other, more legitimate actions; they can or should be able to impose the costs of such suits on those who bring them. Neale and Goyder have made the quite sensible suggestion that the courts be empowered to allow costs against any plaintiff bringing a suit 'in bad faith or vexatiously' – this remedy was made available against state Attorneys-General by the 1976 Antitrust Improvement Act, and could readily be 'extended to the normal antitrust case, so as to conform with the rule for costs under English law'.[32] Indeed, aggrieved competitors or customers who bring unsuccessful antitrust actions under the Export Trading Company Act of 1982 are already required, by that Act, to pay the reasonable attorney fees of the defendant.[33]

Similarly, the charge that damages cannot be measured 'objectively', or with precision, does not justify eliminating the damage

---

31 'Treble damage complaints are now filed in an attempt to intimidate defendants into modifying their conduct in a way favourable to the interests of the plaintiff ... Thus, the new antitrust strategy has achieved its noncompensatory goal.' Arthur D. Austin, 'Negative Effects of Treble Damage Actions: Reflections on the New Antitrust Strategy', Duke L. J., 1978, pp. 1353–4.

32 Op. cit., pp. 435–6.

33 Donald L. Baker, 'Reagan Administration Opens Debate on Treble Damages', 5 The Nat'l L. J., 1983, pp. 20–2.

remedy. GNP and unemployment are not capable of precise measurement, yet we do not abandon efforts to distinguish between recessions and recoveries. And the Chicago School does not seem willing to abandon monetarism simply because it can neither define 'money' nor measure the money supply. As I stated earlier, economists and the courts have done a tolerable job of avoiding both the search for unavailable precision and reliance on sheer guesswork. With greater judicial control in the early stages of cases involving thwarted entrants, further improvement is attainable. Here, as in other areas of the law, we cannot let the perfect be the enemy of the good.

The other criticisms of treble-damage actions are based on the false assumption that the goal of antitrust policy is solely to improve the efficiency with which resources are allocated: 'Since the aim of competition – *and of antitrust policy* – is to achieve an efficient allocation of resources, a plaintiff should not be permitted to recover for the injury from an antitrust violation that does not foster inefficiency.'[34] That is wrong. As Dirlam and Kahn have pointed out:

> Clearly we are not devoted to a competitive system only for
> 'economic' reasons. It is also associated with such social and
> political ideals as the diffusion of private power and
> maximum opportunities for individual self-expression. If
> the economy will run itself, governmental interference in
> our daily life is held to a minimum.[35]

This social purpose includes not only the promotion of efficiency, but of a system perceived to be fair, a concept that 'embod-

---

34 Congressman Webb, p. 504 (emphasis added).

35 Dirlam and Kahn, op. cit., p. 17.

ies values other than those usually conceived by economists in defining maximisation of economic welfare ...'[36] A competitor disadvantaged by some act of a larger rival may indeed seek a solution, at law, that is inconsistent with consumer interests in more output at lower prices. But where has it been decided that conflicts between producers and consumers are to be resolved in favour of the latter? Economists – once proud of the fact that their discipline was known as 'political economy' – should be willing to concede both that they cannot with certainty predict that this or that inefficiency will flow from a given kind of antitrust enforcement and that, since equity is a goal at least equal in importance to efficiency, a wrongful injury to a competitor 'is itself an evil to be avoided'.[37]

In the field of treble damages, this may mean permitting an injured competitor to recover for damages inflicted by a rival's pursuit of what he may feel to be greater efficiency.[38] Just as we cannot be indifferent to theft of property because it merely represents a redistribution of income, a dispute between private parties, so we cannot be indifferent to the 'theft' of business opportunities by powerful from less powerful firms. The wide acceptance accorded to antitrust policy in the United States – described as 'so astonishing' to outsiders[39] – is due to the fact that 'Antitrust has a broader base than the findings of economists as to the conditions required

---

36   Ibid, p. 18.

37   Ibid, p. 206.

38   Critics of treble-damage actions are often sceptical of the claims of injury by individual competitors who may well have lost out to a more efficient rival. Such scepticism is quite proper – and should be applied as well to claims by the victor that his sole intent was the honourable one of long-run profit maximisation, and his competitive weapon greater efficiency.

39   Thorelli, op. cit., p. 442.

for optimum economic performance.'[40] We simply care more that economic power be dispersed, that the economy remain open and fair, than we do that price equal marginal cost – although we quite properly want to know the cost of deviating from optimally efficient solutions.

This can perhaps be made clearer by reference to the current turmoil in our telephone industry. As you know, we have decided – for better or worse – to dismember the Bell System, and to separate the companies providing local telephone service from those doing research, manufacturing equipment and providing long-distance service. This means the more rapid end of the already doomed massive subsidy to local users that has historically been paid by long-distance callers. Economists generally applaud this, but, if they are sensible, *not* because they oppose subsidies as such. Rather, the economist's objection should be to the fact that, given acceptance of universal service as a desirable social goal, the current method of subsidisation is a wasteful and inefficient way of achieving that goal. We certainly can find more efficient ways of achieving that goal than by having long-distance business users saddled with the burden of subsidising unlimited local calls by affluent, chatty teenagers. We can, in other words, accept the *social* goal of universal service and then devise the most efficient means of achieving that objective.[41]

---

40 Ibid, p. 441.

41 For a fuller discussion of these issues see Alfred E. Kahn, 'Some Thoughts on Telephone Access Pricing', based on comments delivered at the Workshop on Local Access: Strategies for Public Policy, St Louis, Missouri, 14–17 September 1982; and Irwin M. Stelzer, 'The Post-Decree Telecommunications Industry', speech delivered before AT&T Long Lines Service Costs and Rates Department Spring Conference, Princeton, New Jersey, 11 May 1982.

This does not mean that we must abandon economic analysis in antitrust cases in order to pursue goals of equity. For, like economic efficiency, equity is an elusive concept:

> Equity in Law, is the same that the Spirit is in Religion, what every one pleases to make it. Sometimes they go according to Conscience, sometimes according to Law, sometimes according to the Rule of Court.
>
> Equity is a Roguish thing: for Law we have a measure, know what to trust to; Equity is according to Conscience of him that is Chancellor, and as that is larger or narrower, so is Equity. 'Tis all one as if they should make the Standard for the measure, we call a Foot, a Chancellor's Foot; what an uncertain Measure would this be? One Chancellor has a long Foot, another a short Foot, a Third an indifferent Foot: 'Tis the same thing in the Chancellor's Conscience.[42]

Rather, the economist must accept the fact that, in the balancing of interests that is the essence of the political process, efficiency must at times be sacrificed to other goals. It then becomes the economist's job to measure that sacrifice, to point it out, to help society make its choice of some non-economic goal in full knowledge of the economic cost associated with that choice.

Fortunately, this conflict between efficiency and equity is not nearly as great or as frequent as is often thought. Most economists agree – as do thoughtful legislators – that, most of the time, competition generates more favourable economic results than any other system. Even where there are economies of scale, it is generally believed (rarely well proved) that the dynamic advantages of

---

42   *The Table-Talk of John Selden*, 1847, p. 49.

competition outweigh all but the very greatest static economies of scale. Thus, by giving consumers a wide range of choices, competition leads to greater *efficiency* in satisfying consumer needs. Equally important, giving choices to consumers is itself an important *social* goal of competition. The general presumption, therefore, is that competition is both more efficient and more socially desirable than monopoly, and that the burden of proof in any given case must rest on the defender of the monopoly if he wants to allege that circumstances make monopoly the preferable industry structure.

For both economic and social reasons, then, our antitrust laws are aimed at preserving the competitive *process* for its own sake, subject only to specified legislative exceptions. The competitive process, with those exceptions noted, is generally believed to be best for the public as a whole. To ensure that the competitive process works properly, the laws are designed to prevent the achievement of monopoly by any means other than those most strictly consonant with competition. The notion of fair competition refers to the kind of competitive process that gives the prize to the firm that operates most efficiently to satisfy public needs. Unfair competitive methods are proscribed by the law to prevent the same kind of distortion of the competitive process that would result were fraud and violence permissible competitive tools.

It seems not unreasonable to conclude our review of the virtues and defects of US treble-damage policy as follows. The availability of this remedy has greatly increased the resources devoted to, and has probably increased the effectiveness of, our antitrust policy. It has also probably led to some useless litigation, a defect which can be corrected by a combination of greater willingness of judges to grant summary motions for dismissal and otherwise control these cases in their early stages,[43] and increased use of the English system of imposing some costs on unsuccessful plaintiffs, and high costs on frivolous ones.

Applicability of US experience to Europe

While it may be the case that the availability of private remedies, and of treble damages, has made an important contribution to the vigour of US antitrust policy, it does not necessarily follow that European competition policy can effectively incorporate this remedy. I would like, now, to explore that question, or at least open it to discussion by those more expert in European competition policy than I.

It seems safe to begin with two assumptions. The first is that, in the end, European policy-makers will decide that increasing the range and vigour of the competitive process is in the public interest. I recognise, of course, that support for competition as a way of business life has far less general acceptance in Europe than in the United States. And pressures from specific industries to sacrifice long-run, dynamic efficiency goals in the interests of short-term job protection will continue to be severe. But the advantages of competition are becoming increasingly obvious – consumers are more restless when their choices are restricted, and opinion leaders increasingly vocal in their opposition to many forms of cartelisation, rationalisation and bars to competitive entry.[*]

---

43 This, of course, is not easy. See note 32 above.

* In the two decades since this talk was delivered, competition policy as practised in Brussels and in Britain has moved considerably closer to the US model, although for EU and UK policy-makers treble-damage recovery remains a step too far in the US direction. Britain is now about to add criminal penalties to the arsenal of weapons available to enforcers of competition policy.

If this attitude in favour of competition prevails, decision-makers in Europe should welcome the additional resources that would be devoted to enforcement if the treble-damage remedy were made widely available to private parties.[44]

A second assumption that seems not unreasonable is that the American interest in preserving the competitive *process* will, on reflection, prove attractive in Europe, and particularly in the UK, precisely because it is a process-oriented rather than a results-oriented approach to economic policy. The entire Anglo-American system is, after all, strongly process-oriented. What we look for is a fair trial, one in which truth and justice will result from the fairness of the *process*. In the field of economics, the competitive process provides the fair trial – in the marketplace rather than in the courtroom. If the rules governing that competitive process are sensible and are enforced, efficiencies will follow. Just as truth and justice cannot be expected to come out of a courtroom in which there is no fair process, efficiency cannot result from an inadequately competitive market process.

But even if these assumptions are correct – even if there is increasing support for European competition policy and for the competitive process – serious problems face those who would urge the adoption of United States treble-damage policy in Europe. First, and most important, is the residual European ambivalence

---

44 Even Professor F. G. Jacobs, sceptical of the role of civil enforcement of EEC anti-trust law, concedes that such enforcement 'will lead to the more effective policing of the EEC competition rules ... The Commission's resources are notoriously over-stretched, and decentralized enforcement might prove speedier and more effective.' F. G. Jacobs, 'Civil Enforcement of EEC Anti-Trust Law', paper delivered at the Second Oxford International Antitrust Law Conference, Queen's College, Oxford 12 September 1983, pp. 6–7 (mimeo).

towards competition as a goal in and of itself.[45] European competition policy is encrusted with other objectives, ranging from expanding the degree of economic integration[46] through the bewildering range of objectives of UK merger policy,[47] objectives which seem to include such exalted goals as 'Keep Sotheby's British'.[48] To permit private parties to recover threefold damages for contravening a vague and unclear set of policies would be quite unfair.[49] On the other hand, the availability of this remedy might itself attract sufficient additional resources to antitrust

45 For an interesting discussion of the wider-than-supposed differences in early English and American attitudes towards competition policy, see William L. Letwin, 'The English Common Law Concerning Monopolies', 21 U. Chi. L. Rev., 1954, pp. 355–85.

46 Why the goals of economic integration and that of achieving effectively competitive markets are at times seen as inconsistent is puzzling. As Wyatt and Dashwood have pointed out, 'It would be futile to require the abolition of customs duties and charges having equivalent effect and of quantitative restrictions and measures having equivalent effect if the isolation of national markets could effectively be maintained by restrictive practices on the part of undertakings, or by State aid policies giving competitive advantages to the national industries.' Derrick Wyatt and Alan Dashwood, *The Substantive Law of the EEC*, 1980, p. 248.

47 Thomas Sharpe has noted that UK competition policy is torn between two opposite views. The one embraces market solutions, accepts 'uncertainty, risk, the promiscuity of the market place'. The other relies on corporatism, a 'belief in co-operation and the brilliance of officials, and in the incapacity of managers to manage in an efficient way and in the national interest'. Remarks at the Second Oxford International Antitrust Law Conference, Queen's College, Oxford, 12 September 1983.

48 Page, op. cit. Sharpe (Note 47 above) has characterised UK merger policy as one in which the 'outer boundary of ministerial discretion is represented by public ridicule'.

49 'It has been pointed out that for such actions, regulations of sufficient clarity would be needed and that the production of such regulations would result in an even more legalistic approach to anti-trust law.' Enric Picanol-Roig, 'Remedies in National Law for Breach of Articles 85 and 86 of the EEC Treaty: A Review', London School of Economics, 1983, p. 50 (mimeo).

enforcement to accelerate the development of a body of case law that would reduce the current vagueness and lack of clarity.

A second problem one faces in urging Europeans to consider permitting private treble-damage actions is that, in order to be effective, that remedy should be coupled with permission for counsel to accept assignments with the fee contingent upon the outcome. I understand from my British friends that such a practice is viewed with horror by the British Bar.* But how else is the penurious plaintiff, unable to finance a lawsuit, to obtain able representation? The somewhat snobbish attitude of old-line American law firms towards the practice is diminishing somewhat, because it has become more respectable for large, blue-chip corporate clients – and, therefore, large, blue-blooded corporate law firms – to be plaintiffs in antitrust proceedings, because even large corporations are trying to develop lower-cost litigation techniques, and because law firms now must compete more vigorously for business, both with other law firms and with in-house law departments. Perhaps European counsel might also want to reconsider their attitudes towards contingent fee arrangements, as part of a reappraisal of the possible advantage of introducing a treble-damage remedy.

Third, one hesitates to recommend importation of this remedy because of the current debate over its efficacy in the United States: an extraordinarily able group of critics, mostly of the Chicago School, is arguing that treble-damage actions have costs far in excess of their benefits.

Finally, one is somewhat cowed by the violence of the parliamentary rhetoric that emerged during the debate over the Protec-

---

* No longer.

tion of Trading Interests Act.[50] During that debate one Conservative member ridiculed American proclivities to export antitrust policy: '. . . the Sherman and Clayton Acts in the United States are the equivalent of holy books . . .' and Americans believe that such 'gospel has to be spread to the pagan and the heathen'.[51] He went on to characterise the treble-damage remedy as 'a well-known device of rather primitive governments who wish to enlist the services of private citizens to police the public order that they think they are unable to police under the public services'.[52] A dispassionate observer can only hope that the high quality of expression does not conceal the considerably lower quality of the underlying logic. First, if one believes in the efficacy of the competitive process, then one has to believe that the laws designed to preserve it are more effectively enforced when many interested parties are allowed to be prosecutors than when the prosecutorial function is placed in the hands of only one. Does anyone seriously consider that it would be appropriate that all breach-of-contract suits be dealt with only by the public prosecutor, rather than by private parties? Does anyone think that individuals should be deprived of the right to sue those who have physically attacked them, even if the public prosecutor decides not to bring the perpetrator to trial?

Second, the implied analogy to the criminal law is inapt. In the criminal law, there are very serious penalties that the public enforcer can impose on a violator: he gets something more than an

---

50 Second Reading, Debate on the Protection of Trading Interests Act of 1983. Hansard (House of Commons) Parliamentary Debate, 15 November 1979, pp. 1553–91, as cited by Donald L Baker, 'U.K. Using New Weapons to Attack Foreign Reach of US Trust Laws', 2 The Nat'l L. J., 1980, p. 24.

51 Ibid.

52 Ibid.

injunction from the court directing the defendant to stop shooting that victim. While it may be adequate in some private antitrust cases to conclude with nothing more than an injunction against continued illegal activity, in cases where the activity in question has already done all of the damage that it can do, only the possibility of penalties can deter the offender and their award compensate the victim. Probably the fairest way to set the size of such penalties is to relate them to the size of the damage done to the victim, and only the private antitrust suit can have any real hope that an appropriate estimate of such damages will be made by the injured party.

These cautions notwithstanding, one is inclined to feel that the right of private parties to bring actions for some multiple of damages inflicted on them by an anti-competitive act, combined with the use of contingent fee arrangements, would have the effect of extending the scope and reach of competition policy in Europe, and soon prompt a clarification of that policy.[53]

These would be substantial advantages.

---

53 But see Jacobs, op. cit., pp. 8, 9. Professor Jacobs sees in the US experience 'a massive misallocation' of legal and other resources'; doubts 'whether even a successful action would do much to promote competition'; and finds that 'It is very doubtful whether such actions are desirable in the public interest . . . '

Changing antitrust standards, with special reference to predation

This talk was delivered at a meeting of the Conference Board in New York City on 5 March 1987, when the bulk of the economics profession had become convinced that there was no such thing as predation, or at least that the instances in which a firm could drive out a competitor and then recoup its losses by barring future entry were extremely rare. I argued that this excessively theoretical approach ignores the real-world fact that potential entrants would note the demise of their predecessor, and refuse to enter into combat with a dominant firm employing predatory pricing and other tactics.

When Tom Campbell* invited me to participate in this programme, I hesitated. Antitrust economics is, after all, a subject that is less well regarded now than it has been – practised by economists who, it is charged, would stifle the upward progress of the economy, prevent American firms from combining to compete against Japan, and encourage greedy plaintiffs' lawyers to seek damages as reimbursement for their clients' inefficiency. Besides, this view continues, since all markets are in the end 'contestable', antitrust enforcement efforts are unnecessary, at best, and counterproductive, at worst. Since I want neither to oppose progress, nor to support the anti-antitrusters, I thought it best to decline.

But Tom is persuasive: he argued, desperately, that I was the only economist he knew who could say *everything* he knew about market power, predation and capital markets in fifteen minutes. Let me try.

---

*   Professor of Law at Stanford University, and until recently a member of the US House of Representatives.

Given the wide acceptance of the view that predation is not a serious problem – indeed, that rational businessmen operating in contestable markets (and most markets are so characterised, these days) would never employ predatory competitive tactics – it is perhaps most instructive to begin by adopting a rebuttal posture, the thesis of which is that the 'there is no such thing as predation' school is wrong for two reasons. The first source of error is the assumption that antitrust policy is concerned solely with questions of economic efficiency. As Joel Dirlam and Alfred Kahn pointed out what now seems long ago:

> Clearly we are not devoted to a competitive system only for 'economic' reasons. It is also associated with such social and political ideals as the diffusion of private power and maximum opportunities for individual self-expression. If the economy will run itself, governmental interference in our daily life is held to a minimum.[54]

This social purpose includes not only the promotion of efficiency, but of a system perceived to be fair, a concept that embodies values other than the maximisation of economic welfare. A competitor disadvantaged by some act of a larger rival may indeed seek a solution, at law, that is unrelated to consumer interests in more output at lower prices, Judge Easterbrook to the contrary notwithstanding. Why not? Economists – once proud of the fact that their discipline was known as 'political economy' – should be willing to concede both that they cannot with certainty predict that this or that inefficiency will flow from a given kind of antitrust enforcement, *and* that, since equity is a goal at least equal in importance to efficiency, a wrongful injury to a competitor is itself an evil to be avoided.

---

54 Dirlam and Kahn, op. cit.

Just as we cannot be indifferent to theft of property because it merely represents a redistribution of income, a dispute between private parties, so we cannot be indifferent to the 'theft' of business opportunities by powerful from less powerful firms. The wide acceptance accorded to antitrust policy in the United States – described as 'so astonishing' by outsiders – is due to the fact that 'Antitrust has a broader base than the findings of economists as to the conditions required for optimum economic performance'.[55] We simply care more that economic power be dispersed, that the economy remain open and fair, than we do that price equal marginal cost – although we quite properly want to know the cost of deviating from optimally efficient solutions.

I recognise, of course, that this notion that efficiency *über alles* is not the goal of antitrust policy is unfashionable, certainly to many Chicago economists and their adherents on the bench. Judge Posner, for example, speaks approvingly of the shift in emphasis of antitrust policy 'from the protection of competition as a process of rivalry to the protection of competition as a means of promoting economic efficiency . . .' (*Olympia Equipment Leasing Co. et al.* v. *Western Union Telegraph Co.*, 797 F.2d 370 (7th Cir. 1986)). If that statement means anything – I am unsure of its meaning because I am uncertain that Judge Posner's sharp distinction between process and result is realistic – it means that efficiency has, by some process of intellectual historical evolution, displaced the once-multiple objectives of antitrust policy, and become the sole goal of such policy. I hope not.

Those who feel that predation is a non-problem err for another reason: even if we assume, with the Chicago School, that

---

55   Neale and Goyder, op. cit.

preservation of efficient competition is the sole goal of antitrust policy, predation can be a threat to the achievement of that goal. This is so for several reasons:

1. Predation is said to be irrational because, in the end, most markets are contestable. Drive out a competitor with below-cost (somehow measured) price cuts, or costly advertising, or some other tactic, and a swarm of new entrants will appear before the forgone profits can be recouped. The uncontestable father of contestability recently stated, in a discussion of the airline industry, that 'Once an incumbent predator attempted to raise its price to make up for an earlier loss, entrants would swarm into the market to take advantage of the opportunity'.[56] Would they? Only if this swarm of entrants, and their backers, were unaffected by the previous practices of the incumbent firm. As I have said before, a hiker might not pay much attention to a no-trespassing sign, standing alone; but if the field behind it is littered with the corpses of previous trespassers, he would most likely decide the sign meant business. And it would matter very little whether the sign had clear legal title to the field.

2. Predation is said to be irrational because it is not profit-maximising behaviour. As I have noted above, predation may, indeed, maximise long-run profits. But assume, for the moment, that it does not. It is not necessary to assume that the business managers who run most modern corporations are irrational or stupid to accept the possibility

---

56   William J. Baumol, 'The Apollo Reservation System and the Public Interest', Before the Civil Aeronautics Board, Docket No. 41686, November 1983, p. 14.

that they will find non-profit-maximising, predatory pricing to be very much in their own interest.

This is so partly because, as Professor Baumol has pointed out, managers will at times prefer to maximise gross sales rather than net profits. It is so also because Berle and Means were right in suggesting that managers, often beyond the reach of the shareholder-owners of the business, may have objectives of their own that have little to do with profit maximisation.

Indeed, as Alfred Kahn has pointed out, it is the Chicagoans who argue – correctly, in my view – that corporate raiders perform a valuable economic function because managements so often fail to adopt that mix of pricing and other practices that would maximise the current discounted values of future revenue streams. It seems to me impossible to argue both (a) that corporate managers are driven to maximise profits and are aware that most markets are sufficiently contestable to make predation irrational, and hence will not engage in predatory pricing; and (b) that corporate managers so often fail to maximise profits that the securities of the companies they run are undervalued, requiring hostile takeovers and the booting of the managers to get these companies back on the profit maximising track.

In short, predation may not maximise profits. But it may nevertheless be a rational, far from unthinkable policy for business managers seeking to maximise their own career opportunities.

3. Finally, predation is a realistic danger because businessmen don't behave in a manner consistent with the simplistic descriptions of the Chicago School. The world does not

consist of businessmen concentrating on pricing policy to the exclusion of other competitive weapons, or coolly comparing profitability with and without a price cut. Rather, it consists of managers in many instances aware that they possess significant market power, and that their actions will affect the future structures of their industries. These managers view pricing policy as only one part of their overall business strategies, which might include, as well, policies aimed at pre-empting markets by expanding capacity, or by developing and exploiting bottlenecks, or by buying competing or, in the case of airlines, business-feeding firms.

Once we accept this fact – that business strategy is a rich mixture of tactics and policies, some aimed at profit-maximising in the static, narrow sense, others at longer-run, dynamic objectives – we begin to understand why economic analysis in antitrust cases most often cannot usefully employ 'bright line' tests: this price is predatory because it falls below some conception of cost, that price is a legitimate competitive response because it does not. Rather, economic analysis, in the context of antitrust cases, involves a detailed understanding of the particular facts in each case: a particular practice can properly be characterised as anti-competitive only after studying it in the entire context of the firm's activities.

This analysis is made more difficult by the complicating need to determine the presence or absence of market power. As our distinguished chairman, Tom Campbell, has pointed out, 'Antitrust law now divides the business world into two types of firms: those with market power and those without.'[57] In short, whether a given

---

57   T. Campbell, *Texas Law Review*, October 1985.

business practice is anti-competitive, a given price cut predatory, depends on the market power of the firm engaging in that tactic. A small, under-financed firm may cut prices to gain market share, but we need spend little time worrying whether that price cut is in any sense predatory. But an identical price cut by a large, well-financed, multi-product firm may indeed be predatory. How can we tell? By an analysis of the entire pattern of the firm's conduct, informed by an examination of intent.[58] Does this mean that there should be a double standard, one by which to judge competitive practices of small firms, and another by which to judge those of firms with market power? Let me answer that question with a question: if, in the course of a minor street altercation, Muhammad Ali[*] punched someone, would the law treat him the same as it would treat me if I did the punching? I think not: his hands are lethal weapons; mine can do little harm to any adversary.

I must confess, in the end, to a feeling of dissatisfaction with this talk. Most economists would be more comfortable telling you that price cuts to a certain level, relative to some conception of cost, are competitive, while others should be proscribed. Very precise, very professional. But they would also have to tell you that they would have great difficulty measuring cost, however defined – goodbye, precision – and that they would have to see whether

---

58   Even contestable market advocates cannot escape the need to look at intent. Baumol (op. cit., p. 13) defines a predatory act as one 'that *(deliberately)* [his parentheses, my emphasis] incurs a short-run loss in order to prevent entry or to drive out competitors ...' And Judge Posner condemns business practice '... *calculated to* [emphasis added: with the intention of?] make consumers worse off in the long run'. *Olympia Equipment Lease Co. et al.* v. *Western Union Telegraph Co.*, 797 F.2d 370 (7th Cir., 1986).

*   At the time of this talk, heavyweight champion of the world, renowned for his powerful punch.

the cuts 'deliberately' (to use Professor Baumol's term) drove firms from business, or were 'calculated to' (Judge Posner's phrase) make consumers worse off in the long run.

So I suppose that I can give you only this vague guidance: significant market power, although far from pervasive in our world of international competition and dynamic technology, can exist – not all markets are contestable. Where a dominant firm has driven rivals from a market, that market becomes less likely to be the scene of a 'contest': small incumbents, potential entrants and providers of capital are capable of learning from experience. Where a firm with market power engages in price cutting or other competitive tactics, those practices should be examined against evidence of intent, market power and the entire pattern of conduct of that firm in the market. Then and only then can one reach a judgement as to whether the broad goals of antitrust policy would best be served by proscribing the practices under review.

If the vagueness of my conclusion inclines you to prefer the apparent precision of Baumol-Areeda-Turner-Posner *et al.*, I will certainly understand. But I would, in that case, urge you to review your position from time to time, keeping in mind the following injunction:

Recent antitrust jurisprudence teaches that rules of law incorporating prevailing economic doctrines have often required revision, and sometimes reversal, after experience reveals the shortcomings of the theory upon which those rules were based. In short, harsh legal rules predicated on economic policy are dangerous because the economic policy may simply be wrong.[59]

---

59 *Cargill Inc. and Excel Corporation* v. *Monfort of Colorado Inc.*, Brief for Royal Crown Cola Co. as *Amicus Curiae*, Supreme Court, October term, 1985, p. 7.

The parameters of product and geographic markets

This lecture was delivered on 18 September 1989 at Emmanuel College, Cambridge, at the eighth Annual Conference on International Antitrust Law. Its aim was to explain how economists attempt to define the area of combat in which competition takes place, and to show that the tools of microeconomic analysis are sufficiently robust to perform this chore so that enforcement authorities can have confidence that they are dealing with alleged anti-competitive acts in a realistic manner.

My assignment today seems relatively straightforward: to tell you how markets are to be defined in antitrust cases. According to the brochure, I am to answer the question 'What is a market?'. To do this, I am to discuss 'delineation of product and market boundaries – the effect of different market structures and fiscal regimes, etc.'. The most encouraging part of that description is the 'etc.', as it gives me licence to interject some interesting material into what I fear is an otherwise turgid subject.

It is important to understand, at the outset, that the process of market definition is rarely an exercise in precision: the tools of economic analysis are not nearly good enough, the available data not nearly exact enough, to permit an honest economist to come up with a definition of a product market so precise that he can be absolutely certain that he has included all reasonable substitutes, and excluded only products that are in no circumstances effective alternatives to the 'product' he has decided upon. Nor can he be precise about the extent of the geographic area within which effective competition is played out. As D. H. Robertson pointed out over 65 years ago, 'The Theory of Economics ... is a method rather than a doctrine, an apparatus of the mind, a technique of thinking, which helps its possessor to draw correct conclusions.'[60]

This should come as no surprise to even the most casual readers of the financial press. Economists specialising in macroeconomic analysis can no longer measure the level of economic activity (revisions often swamp original estimates) or define the rate of inflation (should it include or exclude mortgage rates?). They cannot define 'money', and don't know whether higher interest rates restrain inflation by discouraging spending, or accelerate it by raising costs and by encouraging higher wage demands. They can't even decide whether government revenue can be increased by raising taxes, or by lowering them.

Yet when the context is litigation, or in this country the variety of informal proceedings that substitute for that much-despised American art form, all of that is ignored. Lawyers, administrators and judges want economists to define markets, identify sources of market power, predict whether a merger will lessen competition and otherwise wring from often conflicting data answers that permit them to make important policy decisions.

Fortunately, the tools of microeconomic analysis are so superior to those of macroeconomic analysis that it is possible for me to present a framework within which those questions can be answered.

I will do so, first, by describing how the product and geo-

---

60 D. H. Robertson, *The Control of Industry*, The Mayflower Press, William Brendon & Son, Ltd, Plymouth, 1923 (reprinted and revised 1936), p. v. Robertson went on to note, 'The main task of the professional economist now consists, either in obtaining a wide knowledge of relevant facts and exercising skill in the application of economic principles to them, or in expounding the elements of his method in a lucid, accurate and illuminating way ...' Today's mathematical economists please note.

graphic dimensions of a 'market' can be defined. This will be of some use to those of you new to the subject, and of little use to those among you who are experienced antitrust practitioners. Second, I will describe how an economist gathers the information he needs to inform his judgement. Third, I will discuss a dimension of market structure that has attracted attention recently – the structure of companies' finances. Finally, I will offer a few comments on the value of the entire exercise.

Defining a market

The object of defining a relevant market is to determine the arenas within which effective competition occurs or, conversely, market power is exercised. In order to make such a determination, several dimensions of the competitive arena must be delineated.

First, the *product* engaged in the competitive battle must be defined: is the market battle one of tin can v. tin can, or tin cans v. all containers; is the fight between coal from different mines, or between all fuels? Second, the contestants must be identified: who are the actual and potential suppliers of the product in question? Third, we must know where the arena is, its geographic dimension: is the fight between domestic companies only, or are foreigners effective contestants for the consumer's favour? Finally, all of these analyses must have a time dimension: substantial short-term monopoly power may melt away in the face of changes in the product and geographic dimensions of a market resulting from adaptations by existing firms; entry; or changes in technology, government regulation, or consumer tastes and preferences.

A product market can be defined as a set of goods or services that represent reasonable alternatives to one another. In America, that is now taken to mean goods or services sufficiently alike so that 'a significant and nontransitory price increase (usually five per cent for one year)' would drive enough customers to use a substitute so as to make such a price increase unprofitable.[61]

A *geographic* market sets the boundary 'that roughly separates producers that ... would frustrate an attempt by a firm or firms to exercise market power' from those too distant to do so.[62]

Let me expand a little on each of those dimensions of the market – the product, and the geographic area.

a. Product market

A product market includes all goods that, in the view of consumers, are realistic substitutes, one for the other. The suppliers of these goods include all producers currently producing and selling, and/or realistically able to produce and sell, in the product market.

The definition of demand substitutability should not be so broad as to include products that are only remotely possible substitutes for one another, but should include goods or services consumers actually substitute for one another, or could easily substitute. Economists do not define product markets in terms of isolated instances of substitutability; nor do they require that substitutability be universal, that is, applicable to all consumers. Rather, we look to consumer reactions sufficient to affect suppliers' pricing and production decisions. What guides the behaviour

---

61 See US Department of Justice Antitrust Division, 'Antitrust Enforcement Guidelines for International Operations', 10 November 1988, p. 39. This definition is offered in the context of merger analysis, but works well enough for our purposes.

62 Ibid.

of those firms is the possibility that customers, faced with higher-than-competitively-determined prices, will choose to substitute lower-priced alternatives realistically available in the market. Of course, not *every* customer will be willing to switch brands or find alternatives when prices are raised. But it is the presence of a significant number who are willing to make such substitutions that will guide the conduct of sellers in the market. We are, in other words, interested in competition at the margin, in the presence of a significant number of each firm's customers for whom there are realistic substitutes for that firm's product.

Competing in this product market are all the firms that supply that product or that could do so 'easily and economically', to use the words of the Antitrust Division.[63] In the short run, this would include all firms having the ability to supply the product in question, using existing personnel and equipment. In the longer term we would include all firms with ultimate ability to shift from the supply of one good to supplying the product in question by adding at least some significant new equipment or new personnel.

b. Geographic market

A geographic market, like a product market, is defined to include the area over which consumers can realistically turn for alternative sources of substitute products and over which alternative suppliers realistically can make the product available. In this connection, many of the considerations applicable to product market definition apply here as well: substitutability must be a realistic option – given the prevailing economic and institutional environment – for

---

63   Ibid, p. 40.

suppliers to be included in a given geographic market. They must, for example, be able not only to manufacture the goods in question, but to market and distribute them. And profitably.

Lest this description leave a question in anyone's mind about whether imports should be included in the definition of a relevant product and geographic market, I would like to answer that question with an economist's version of an unequivocal answer: perhaps.

If there are tariff or other barriers that effectively exclude foreign products, those products do not constrain the pricing behaviour of domestic producers and should be excluded from the market definition. And if procurement policies do not permit imports, such imports are not a competitive factor and should be excluded. But if imports can and likely will flow into a country in response to a given price increase by domestic firms, those imports are properly included in any realistic market definition. As Sir Gordon Borrie has said, '... competition – and potential competition – from imports' are part of any 'examination of how far the market is "contestable".'[64] This position parallels that of America's authorities: the Justice Department's latest merger guidelines, unlike their predecessor, 'allow specifically for the possibility of imputing market share to potential foreign suppliers ...'[65]

c. The time dimension

All of the competition to which we are referring must occur within a given time dimension. For purposes of convenience, the US Anti-

---

64 Sir Gordon Borrie, 'Merger Policy: Current Policy Concerns', in James A. Fairburn and John A. Kay, *Mergers & Merger Policy*, Oxford University Press, Oxford, 1989, p. 254.

65 George Hay, 'Mergers Policy in the US', in Fairburn and Kay, op. cit., p. 241.

trust Division suggests that substitutes that can effectively be available within one year to dampen price increases be included in product and geographic markets, and that the 'competitive significance' of firms that can enter within two years of a price increase also be considered.[66]

d. UK compared with US

Note that I have, until this point, been relying on thinking in America. This is not due to excessive provincialism. Rather, it is because our antitrust authorities have, until recently, been more explicit than yours on the subject of market definition. That situation may be changing. This summer's White Paper[67] by the Secretary of State for Trade and Industry begins to sketch a British position on this complex subject.

The White Paper makes the optimistic assumption that 'What is the "relevant market" for a particular product or service will be established through economic analysis'.[68] Factors to be considered will include 'normal patterns of supply'; 'the availability of substitutes'; and 'barriers to entry' – all factors referred to by the Department of Justice.

The principal difference is that America's antitrust authorities have a compulsion to seem explicit, while Britain's have an equal compulsion to seem flexible. In fact, the substantive difference is not great. Our Department of Justice, in its 86-page report on antitrust guidelines for international operations, included 299 footnotes,

---

66 Ibid.
67 Department of Trade and Industry, *Opening Markets: New Policy on Restrictive Trade Practices*, HMSO, London, July 1989. Hereinafter, White Paper.
68 Ibid, p. 8.

many of these constituting qualifications of clear sentences in the text. So, too, in the Antitrust Division's *Merger Guidelines*: the text defines as the offending 'small but significant and nontransitory price increase' a 5 per cent rise lasting one year. This it dubs 'an objective standard'. But read footnote seven: a larger increase 'may be appropriate' in some circumstances.[69]

So it is not unfair to say that the authorities in both countries are heading in the same direction, using maps of differing degrees of detail. But they are aboard very different vehicles. The American authorities are making decisions within the context of litigation or, in the case of mergers, potential litigation. Britain's competition policy is enforced, if that is the correct word, by a series of hints, nudges, meetings and other devices opaque to the outsider.[*] This has the advantage of expedition – and of preventing the importation of American-style litigation, a barbarism feared as much in some circles as American-style television, American-style airline deregulation and American-style fast food – all objects of derision by the élite – and sources of delight to British consumers.

Market structure

Having defined the products to be included in a market, and its geographic scope, the next step is to identify the firms operating in that market, a subject to which I have already alluded.

---

69 US Department of Justice Antitrust Division, *Merger Guidelines*.
*   The UK process has become more structured. But direct confrontation by parties to a dispute is still not considered useful or acceptable, and the ability of companies unhappy with the authorities' decisions to appeal to the courts is severely limited.

The universe should, as we have said, include firms already serving the market, and firms 'that could easily and economically do so' in a reasonable period of time. Clearly, that involves an appraisal of ease of entry, which in turn involves a host of considerations: the length of life of assets; the availability of distribution facilities; the presence or absence of excess capacity.

That small chore done, we then have (1) a definition of the products contesting for consumers' favour; (2) a delineation of the geographic area in which the contest is being fought; and (3) a list of the contestants.

That information in hand, we can proceed to a description of the structure of the market. The most significant structural features considered are the current degree of concentration (the portion of total sales capacity, assets, etc., accounted for by the largest firms operating in a given market); the degree of dispersion in market shares among the market's participants, e.g. as measured by the Hirschman-Herfindahl Index (HHI);[70] trends in concentration over time (changes in the size distribution of existing firms and the extent of entry and exit); the height of barriers to entry (the disadvantages of potential entrants vis-à-vis established firms); and the structure of customer and factor markets (the market power possessed by suppliers to and customers of the market under investigation). Other factors, such as the physical characteristics of the product itself (e.g. perishability, weight, fungibility) are often considered under the 'market structure' heading.

---

70 The HHI is the sum of the squares of the market shares of all participant firms.

Data gathering

To list the ingredients of a market structure analysis is easy. To gather data on each dimension is not. Consider the question posed in America: will a 5 per cent price increase attract so many new competitors as to prove unprofitable? I suspect that most businessmen would pay a great deal for the answer to that question – whether or not they were faced with an antitrust challenge.

Or think about responding to the challenge laid down in the White Paper. The DTI suggests that 'In a complex case, evidence of the degree of response in the demand for one product, given changes in its price relative to that of another, might be brought to demonstrate' the extent of the availability of substitutes and of barriers to entry.[71]

The first problem, of course, is that data are usually not readily available to permit many of the computations needed.[72] Or are not available for a recent year. Or for potential as well as existing competitors. Or for historic price movements.

So one must make do with such data as one can get, supplemented by the all-important set of trade press and industrial documents that permit the discerning analyst to get a sense of what the business being examined is all about. Recall that I began this talk with a reference to D. H. Robertson's long-ago admonition that the 'main task of the professional economist' includes 'a wide knowledge of *relevant* facts'. Those facts can, in America, be obtained by the process of discovery.

---

71 White Paper, p. 8.

72 In America, for example, industry data published by the Bureau of the Census are often not in a form 'designed solely or even primarily to support definitions of markets'. James W. McKie, 'Market Definition and the SIC Approach', in Franklin M. Fisher (ed.), *Antitrust and Regulation*, MIT Press, Cambridge, MA, 1985, p. 85.

That process, at least in American antitrust cases (and apparently in British securities fraud cases), is so time-consuming, so expensive, that it often appears to be an end in itself for dominant firms and otherwise underemployed antitrust lawyers in both the public and private sectors. So I hesitate to point out that it might, after all, have some small use in reaching a conclusion or two. Discovery should reveal how firms in an industry perceive their markets, and who they perceive to be their major competitors. If IBM follows the activities of firm A, it must feel that it is a competitor; if it monitors the performance of product X, it must feel that X is in one of its own product markets. Does it monitor developments in the Japanese abacus, or in disk drives? All of these facts rest in company files – sometimes in deliciously detailed competitive market reports.[73]

Another approach, of course, is to attempt to develop econometric measures of the cross-elasticities of demand between products, to see if those cross-elasticities are high enough to make price increases unprofitable in one of the product markets, i.e. if, for purposes of analysis of the force of competition, the apparently separate products belong in one product market. The DTI hopes that 'in the majority of cases' such an analysis will prove unnecessary, because 'the relevant market should readily be capable of identification'.[74] Perhaps. But if my dictionary is correct in defining 'readily' as 'without difficulty' I am sceptical.

This does not mean that I think that econometric studies of demand elasticity will become the principal tool of market definition. But I do think that the chore of defining markets will

---

73 Unfortunately, distinguishing between company documents that reliably report real-world happenings, and those that reflect the wilder imaginings of sales managers, is itself an art.

74 White Paper, p. 8.

not be an easy one. Let me illustrate by reference to a highly controversial study in which I have very recently participated: that of the media business.

An example

The task was complicated, first, by the fact that competition in the business is two-dimensional: media firms compete for audiences, and for advertisers. Furthermore, these markets are interrelated: to compete successfully for advertisers, a newspaper or a broadcaster must have an audience.

A second complication arose from the difficulty of defining the product. Is there a market for media, with print and electronic delivery systems competing with one another? Or is print a separate product? And, within the print business, do national and regional newspapers compete with one another? And with magazines? Or are these separate markets?

I won't bore you with the details of our analysis: I can provide copies to anyone interested.[75] It suffices for my purposes here to cite three conclusions that are applicable to most studies. First, the data available are imperfect; second, dynamic technologies make change so rapid that any snapshot of the situation is necessarily a bit blurred; and, third, notwithstanding these difficulties, an economist can develop a reasonably realistic picture of the nature and vigour of competition in media markets by discovering the collapse of entry barriers, the absence of power over prices, and the intensity of the rivalry for advertisers and audience.

---

75 See News International plc, 'Competition, Diversity and Cross-Media Ownership', August 1989.

Leverage

No discussion of market structure would be complete these days without some mention of leverage, and its use in hostile takeovers, if for no other reason than that such takeovers now seem to dominate discussions of merger policy. This is, of course, in sharp contrast to the concerns that once dominated such discussion. Until very recently, merger policy in most countries was designed to examine friendly mergers – the voluntary coming together of firms that had once been rivals. This was the case with most mergers proposed in the Britain of the 1960s, when mergers were consummated in an effort to gain the benefits thought to accrue to size.[76]

The acquisitions of the 1980s have the opposite purpose: to de-merge, or deconglomerate, or otherwise shrink large, often diversified firms on the theory that the value of the sum of the parts exceeds the whole.

I won't here try to persuade you to agree with my view, and those of many academics and businessmen, that such hostile takeovers and the threat of such takeovers are an important goad to efficiency. I state that conclusion merely to alert you to what some of you might consider my bias.

But I do want to consider the effect government actions to prevent highly leveraged, hostile takeovers might have on competition. It seems to me self-evident that such rules would reduce competition in two important markets.

The first of these is the market for corporate control. Leverage permits the likes of entrepreneurs such as Goldsmith, Murdoch

---

76 They apparently resulted in 'an industrial structure which neither public nor business policy would now wish to put together'. Fairburn and Kay, op. cit., pp. 6, 15.

and others to vie for the control of existing assets in opposition to incumbent managers. Such competition, whatever else it does, produces the same pressures for efficiency and maximum earnings as does the more traditional competition among producers operating in a relevant product and geographic market.

The second form of competition that the imposition of arbitrary limitations on leverage would stifle is the competition of the potential entrant. So long as vigorous entrepreneurs can enter, or threaten to enter, a market using borrowed funds made available by informed lenders, existing firms must worry – and offer good products, at reasonable prices, while earning profits satisfactory to investors.

So, at least from a competition policy perspective, limitations on borrowings by potential entrants should be avoided.

The values of market structure analysis

I have now bored you for almost as long as any reasonable person would consider decent. And I fear I must conclude with the admission that your time may have been poorly spent. For I am not at all certain that exercises in defining markets are very useful – at least taken alone.

Recent developments in economic analyses support a view long held by more sophisticated antitrust economists: that the determinants of the competitiveness of a market include far more than the number of firms that occupy it, or the concentration in that market.[77] Even firms in highly concentrated industries, pro-

---

77 See Joseph E. Stiglitz and G. Frank Mathewson (eds), *New Developments in the Analysis of Market Structure*, MIT Press, Cambridge, MA, 1986, especially p. xv; and G. C. Archibald, B. C. Eaton and R. G. Lipsey, 'Address Models of Value Theory', pp. 3–47.

tected by 'insurmountable barriers to entry', may not 'agree on a mutually acceptable cooperative outcome' in the absence of what we call 'facilitating devices'.[78]

So market *structure* information tells a highly incomplete story about market *power*. The structure statistics might tell you the current portion of the defined market occupied by a firm, and the trend in that share. But they alone cannot give an unambiguous indication of the presence of market power because they do not tell enough about the power to exclude, to erect barriers to entry.[79] A firm with 70 per cent of the market, down from 95 per cent a few years earlier, may have less market power than one with a stable 60 per cent share (although both may have substantial power). Two firms, in different industries, may have high market shares, the one because of economies of scale, the other because of preclusively high advertising budgets. The structure statistics shed little light on these problems – the presence and sources of market power. For an economist to conclude that high market *share* means market *power* he must, first, look to the causes of that high share. And here he must rely on a detailed analysis of the documents and explanations of the firm's business methods and conduct over time – no small chore. Unless counsel makes it possible for his expert to do that, he will be left with a record which reads as follows:

---

78 Steven C. Salop, 'Practices that (Credibly) Facilitate Oligopoly Co-ordination', in Stiglitz and Mathewson, op. cit., p. 265.

79 'We are certainly far from being able to predict with absolute certainty that an increase in concentration will have precise and quantifiable adverse effect on competition, or on performance.' John H. Shenefield, 'Antitrust Policy – Populist Philosophy or Economic Necessity?', remarks before the Los Angeles County Bar Association, 30 January 1978, p. 6 (mimeo).

Q. What share of the relevant market is occupied by the Scoundrel Timepiece Corporation we here seek to break up?
A. 80 per cent.
Q. For what year is that statistic?
A. 1970, the last for which data are available.
Q. Has anything happened since then that might have affected that figure?
A. Other than a flood of imports, the development of digital watches and a price war, nothing comes to mind – so I'll stick with my 80 per cent.
Q. What conclusion do you draw from that 80 per cent?
A. Eight out of ten watches sold in 1970 were made by Scoundrel Timepiece Corporation.
Q. Anything else – please?
A. There may be terrible political consequences of such power.
Q. Did you say 'power'?
A. Sorry: I meant to say high market share.
Q. What about power?
A. That's a different question.

Clearly, not very persuasive. What is required, in addition, is an examination of behaviour, particularly with respect to price. The fundamental difference between a firm with monopoly power and one without such power is power over price. The firm with monopoly power can choose the price that it wishes to charge, given the demand characteristics of the market in question and the monopolist's perceptions of the behaviour of its existing rivals and potential entrants. The firm with monopoly power can set a high price, relative to its costs, to maximise its profits. Or the monopoly firm may charge a very low price in an effort to drive rivals out of the market or discourage entry into the market in the hope that the associated reduction in competition will allow it to charge much higher prices in the future. The firm with monopoly power and substantial resources might even charge prices so low that it loses money, driving smaller, equally efficient firms from the market, financing the losses from its cash hoard, all with the hope of charging much higher prices in the future when competition has either been eliminated or constrained.[80]

Substantial power over price is the fundamental characteristic of a firm possessing monopoly power. Find that and you can spare yourself a great deal of anguished analysis of market structure statistics.

---

80 It is, of course, the current fashion in the economic literature to deny the possibility of such predatory pricing. But see my 'Changing Antitrust Standards', comments at the Workshop on Antitrust Issues in Today's Economy, *The Conference Board*, 5 March 1987, reprinted on pp. 43–50 of this volume.

Market power and competition in the age of technology

The following lecture was delivered at a meeting of the Federalist Society for Law and Public Policy in Washington, DC, on 14 November 1998, at a time when the Microsoft case was in full contention, in the courts and in the think tanks and the academic press. Query: has the emergence of a 'new' high-tech economy made the antitrust laws obsolete?

It is important to approach the subject of 'Market Power and Competition in the Age of Technology' with some care – for two reasons. First, while there are many important American industries that can be classified as 'high-tech' by one definition or another, many have not changed very much in recent years in those aspects that are important to makers of competition policy. Automobiles may be produced by robots, and the geographic reach of suppliers in our increasingly 'globalised economy' may have increased in recent decades, but neither of these changes suggests that traditional antitrust policy, which includes economically sensible definitions of markets, needs revision. So, too, with oil, cement, steel and other important components of America's present-day economy. In short, we may be in 'The Age of Technology', but it is an age that requires review of competition policy as applied to some, not all, industries, despite the efforts of all industries to argue that they are indeed candidates for inclusion in the new high-tech world in which competition policy can be relaxed or, better still, suspended.

Second, it is important to remember that almost every change in the circumstances in which our industries operate has led those who have never met an antitrust case they like to call for a major revision – read, relaxation – of competition policy.

- When the nation found itself in the throes of the great depression, many policy-makers urged that the solution to the perceived ills – low prices and high unemployment – was a relaxation or repeal of the laws that prevented businesses from conspiring to raise prices and moderate the pace of the introduction of what were seen as job-destroying new technologies.

- When some markets became more global, we were told that the antitrust laws had become obsolete; never mind that traditional antitrust policy can easily accommodate in its definition of relevant markets – the geographic arena in which competition is occurring – an expansion of the scope of the market in the light of changed circumstances that may broaden the area from which consumers may draw the product in question.

- When faced with a cartel of oil-producing nations, and temporary supply cut-offs, we were told that the antitrust laws were impediments to our ability to cope with the new geopolitics of energy; if only the oil companies could be freed from the shackles that prevented them from co-operating – read, colluding – all would be well.

Now we are faced with the emergence of a host of new industries that have as their principal assets something known as 'intellectual property', created by entrepreneurs whose youth and ability to convert the future potential of their ideas into instant fortunes through the magic of IPOs have propelled them to the covers of the leading business magazines, where we see the faces of young, jeans-clad, mother-and-apple-pie businessmen smiling out at us. No scowling J. P. Morgan or J. D. Rockefeller, watch chains gleaming on buttoned-up waistcoats, to suggest greed and a whiff of evil.

Add to the benign image surrounding the creators of the new technology the new emphasis on international competitiveness. Never mind that Paul Krugman[*] and other economists have debunked the notion that the concept of rivalry among firms can be translated into a theory of rivalry among nations – international trade, after all, is not a zero-sum game. The popular perception is that America is in a struggle for survival, and that the troops on which it must rely in this commercial battle are the creators of intellectual property. After all, the Japanese proved that we cannot rely on our auto industry, the Koreans and Russians are proving that our steel industry is not up to the battle, and the Chinese and others are in a position to send our apparel industry to the same graveyard in which rests our shoe industry. So we must rely on our high-tech industries to preserve our international economic position, and anything that interferes with the ability of those industries to operate free from government oversight is against the public interest.

I would like to persuade you that all of the developments that I have just discussed make vigorous enforcement of the antitrust laws more, rather than less, crucial to the continued success of the American economy, and to the preservation of the social values that underpin our entrepreneurial economy – that to go 'soft' on antitrust would be bad public policy.[81]

In a world in which intellectual capital is rapidly replacing

---

[*] Professor of Economics at MIT, and a columnist for the *New York Times*.

[81] The following half-dozen paragraphs rely on John H. Shenefield and Irwin M. Stelzer, *The Antitrust Laws: A Primer*, AEI Press, Washington, DC, 1998 (third ed.), pp. 81–3.

physical capital as the cornerstone of the wealth of nations, nothing can be more important than getting the application of the antitrust laws to intellectual property right. That is no easy chore. Intellectual property is developed both by corporate research departments and the fabled lone inventor working in his garage in response to the prospects of substantial rewards. The risks that a research effort will come to naught, that some other inventor will beat the putative innovator to the finish line, that an invention or innovation will seem feasible in the laboratory but prove too costly or perhaps even impossible to produce in marketable quantities, all point to the need to protect intellectual property so that its owner can reap his just rewards.

Unfortunately, the level of those rewards is directly related to the innovator's ability to deprive others of the use of his invention or trade secret. Make the intellectual property available to all who would use it, and you hasten its introduction; but at the same time you seriously reduce the incentive to create such property in the first place. It is this tension between the desire to encourage invention, innovation and the on-going march of technology and productivity, and the desire to maximise the diffusion of new discoveries, that the antitrust laws must accommodate.

The first of these goals—maximising the pace of innovation—calls for the absolute protection of intellectual property rights. To the extent that an innovator cannot appropriate to himself the benefits of his work, his incentive to struggle on is diminished. When 'free riders' can use the results without sharing in the costs of research and development, the private sector will invest less in research than is in the nation's interest. So we have laws granting innovators the absolute right to the fruits of their efforts, laws that provide for the patenting of inventions and the perpetual protection of trade secrets.

The second goal – rapid diffusion of new inventions and techniques – is met in two ways. The law permits the inventor to gain the benefits of economies of scale by licensing his invention to others, thereby spreading the fixed costs of research and development over the output of those licensees. At the same time it protects his stake in his invention by permitting him to restrict licensees' use of his work in any way that maximises its value. Without such a guarantee, the inventor's incentive to license his work to others would be diluted.

Equally important, rapid diffusion of innovation is assured by preserving a competitive marketplace. The developer of a new product or process may wish to control the pace at which those innovations are introduced, and to maintain the price of the product or process at a level that yields monopoly profits. But he must always reckon with the possibility that some equally talented innovator or equally well-funded research laboratory will come up with a superior product, or a more efficient method of production. And that the antitrust laws will ensure that channels of distribution are not unfairly denied, and that those with a stake in the status quo cannot use their market power or conspire with others to make it difficult for the new product to obtain such manufacturing and financial support as it may be able to command in an open marketplace.

These policy goals can be achieved only if the antitrust laws are applied in all their aspects to high-tech as well as to low-tech industries.

- A firm with substantial market power, even power fairly won in the marketplace, cannot be allowed to leverage that power by tying other products to the one that it dominates.

- A firm with substantial market power cannot be allowed to use that power to bludgeon independent manufacturers not to deal with its competitors, or impose a pricing system that accomplishes that same result.
- A firm with substantial market power over a product, access to which is crucial for firms that compete with it in other product markets, cannot be allowed to deny access unless potential competitors agree to cede other markets to it.

Surely, nothing in the nature of high-tech industries obviates these long-standing policy truths. Indeed, they seem to me more compelling in the case of industries in which waves of creatively destructive innovation are to be relied on as the principal engines of progress. In many of these industries, newcomers – the pizza-eating graduate student with a bright idea and a zero bank balance – rely on venture capitalists for the seed capital needed to take their ideas from concept to marketable product. These venture capitalists are notably hard-headed realists. If they believe that an entrenched incumbent will be allowed to snuff out incipient competition by inducing manufacturers to boycott the new product, or by using technological legerdemain to tie its own competing product to its monopoly product, venture capitalists will suggest to the newcomer that completion of his doctoral dissertation or a job with the entrenched incumbent is his best option.

So I would urge you to think long and hard before jumping to the conclusion that we must abandon the competition policy that has contributed so much to the growth of the American economy, and conferred on us the socially stabilising consequences of a policy that promises the upwardly mobile a fair field with no favours. Of course, antitrust policy will have to be applied with the economic sense that has enabled it to remain a viable tool for the preservation of competition for over a century. That will require that at least two areas of application be applied with sensitivity.

- If it is indeed the case that high-tech products have short economic lives, that fact will have to be factored into any appraisal and measurement of market power. Antitrust policy has never been aimed at demonstrably transient market power, and there is no reason to fear that it will be in the future, especially since enforcement agencies have learned what some take to be the generalisable lesson of the protracted IBM case.
- The question of relief will have to be given even greater consideration in the future than in the past. The notion that the antitrust laws are proscriptive rather than prescriptive is less compelling than it once was: if an enforcement agency doesn't know what remedy to propose, it should stay its hand. And that remedy cannot require on-going judicial supervision of the practices of a company specialising in the creation of intellectual property, for the obvious reason that we do not want to slow the pace of innovation to accommodate the more leisurely one of the judicial process. This may mean that relief will have to be more radical in the case of high-tech violators of the antitrust laws than in the case of lower-tech ones, with divestiture and structural solutions playing a larger role relative to the prohibition of specific practices. Application of this policy to the Microsoft case would require the company, if it has done what it is accused of having done, to spin off its operating system. That would surely be more efficient than burdening judges with

the chore of deciding which products are intrinsic parts of that system, and which are separate products being entangled in the operating system merely or primarily to stifle competition.

I do hope these brief remarks will persuade you that the policies that have stood us in such good stead in the past can, if applied with economic nous, serve us well in the future. After all, if Judge Robert Bork, one of the nation's leading antitrust scholars, is persuaded that the laws that are applicable to old-economy newspapers are equally applicable to new-economy Microsoft, we should surely hesitate before concluding that the world has so changed that price fixing, tying, boycotts and other practices are unexceptionable, so long as they are practised only by high-tech firms.

Comments on competition policy

The Institute of Economic Affairs has the delightful practice of scheduling 'working lunches' at which interested parties exchange views on a variety of topics, after brief remarks by an invited speaker. On 18 May 2000 I led off the discussion with these comments.

I would like to make five points this afternoon:

1. Vigorous competition policy, one that seems on its surface to be anti-business, is good public policy.
2. Penalties under the new UK Competition Act are insufficiently severe to discourage a large number of violations.
3. The new emphasis on consumer protection is unnecessary and may be counterproductive.
4. It is especially important that competition policy be vigorously pursued in the so-called 'high-tech' industries, and that structural rather than procedural remedies be used when anti-competitive behaviour rears its ugly head in these industries.
5. People matter.

Let me treat those points in order:

1. *Vigorous competition policy is good public policy* for several reasons. First, by preventing incumbent firms from conspiring to share markets and keep out intruders, and by preventing dominant firms from using their market power to exclude new entrants, it encourages entrepreneurship and risk-taking. Newcomers know that they will have recourse if prevented from competing on their merits with existing firms.

This general tone, this spirit that all is possible, contributes importantly to a culture that denies protection to those unable to win favour in the marketplace, on the assumption that the opportunities offered by a growing and open economy are a better cure for the problems of those who lose the competitive race than are government subsidies.

So your Chancellor is quite right in linking vigorous competition policy to risk-taking, to economic dynamism, and to rapid innovation.

Second, and related to the first advantage, vigorous competition policy contributes to social mobility, to a sense that no one is doomed to live out life in the same economic circumstances as did his or her parents. This, in turn, minimises any sense of 'class', and the accompanying resentments that plague societies in which those born at the top of the heap are assured that that is where they will stay.

Finally, vigorous competition policy is good public policy because it prevents the accumulation and abuse of monopoly power, thereby eliminating the need for direct government regulation of prices and output. Where the invisible hand operates, the heavy hand of government is not necessary to establish prices that yield a competitive return and no more. Where competition is absent – where monopoly exists either because dominant firms have used their power to exclude competitors, or because an industry is a 'natural monopoly' – direct regulation will inevitably be called upon to protect consumers from extortion. Regulation, we all know, has its place in any capitalist economy: but its place should be limited to instances in which competition policy cannot produce effective competition.

These advantages of a successful competition policy are

important to keep in mind because it has become fashionable to think of competition policy as having a single objective: the maximisation of economic efficiency. At least in the American context, that is incorrect. As John Shenefield and I point out in our little book (*The Antitrust Laws: A Primer*), in our country the goals of antitrust policy include the diffusion of private power and maximisation of opportunities for individual enterprise. These are social/political goals – murky in concept, difficult in application, but very real bases for American antitrust policy.

So much for the advantages of a vigorous competition policy – it prevents the accretion of monopoly power, thereby performing both an economic function (the efficient allocation of resources) and a social function (markets open to thrusting newcomers). If the captains of industry are annoyed, if some choose to call this government interference, so be it.

2. *Current remedies are inadequate to discourage many violations of the law.* Let me now spend a moment on my second point – that Britain's new competition policy, although a much greater deterrent to anti-competitive behaviour than the predecessor regime, is still not tough enough.

Start with penalties. Much has been written about the huge penalties that might be faced by those found to be engaging in anti-competitive behaviour. I would agree, of course, that such fines, and the threats of 'dawn raids', will have some effect on the propensity of business executives to fix prices and otherwise undermine market forces. But in the case of price-fixing conspiracies, large fines are a less effective deterrent than small jail sentences. In America, it is the threat of a stretch as a guest of the government that keeps many an executive out of a smoke-filled room (actually, price fixers probably now meet in the smoke-free environments of various hotel suites) in which prices can be discussed and co-ordinated.

Britain has no such deterrent, which is doubly surprising now that your Home Secretary* has decided that miscreants should be jailed only by day, and then let loose at night. Just as this will free garden-variety crooks such as burglars and muggers to pursue their trade after a day's rest and three square meals at the government's expense, so would this regime leave executives convicted of price fixing free to complete their social and dinner commitments.

Seriously, I believe you will find that it will be a long while before mere fines will destroy the culture of price fixing that permeates British business.

And I doubt, too, that the threat of damage suits, as provided for in the new Act, will be an effective deterrent. As I understand it, an injured party can bring a suit to recover damages. If he wins, the miscreant pays back his ill-gotten gains – and no more. Given that the probability of being sued is less than one, and that the probability that the complainant will prevail is also less than one, it pays to chance paying such damages – nothing to lose, and all to gain. In America, of course, damages are trebled, so that a violator of the law must reckon that he might indeed lose a great deal if he is found to have illegally injured a competitor.

3. *Consumer protection is the wrong goal.* I start with the premise that the ultimate protection consumers have is choice – a variety of competitors vying for their patronage. If we get the rules right, and if the right rules produce the effectively competitive market

---

* Jack Straw at the time of this talk.

structures that we have every reason to expect that they will, if advertisers are not prohibited from hawking their wares, and if the anti-fraud laws are enforced, consumers are amply protected. To raise consumer protection to a separate policy objective has two disadvantages.

First, it invites government to opine on which prices it deems just, and which unjust; and it invites government to squander scarce resources hunting for 'rip-offs' in competitively structured industries.

Second, the notion that consumers need more from government than the preservation of competitive markets (or the regulation of prices in those markets in which competition is unattainable) encourages consumers to look to government rather than to their own knowledge and skill as their ultimate protector. British consumers are in the process of learning that they can protect themselves by voting with their dollars and their feet; they should not now be told that government will take over the chore of seeing to it that they receive quality products at reasonable prices.

4. *Vigorous enforcement of competition law is especially important in new, high-tech industries*. It has become fashionable, especially in conservative circles, to profess amazement that something as old-fashioned as antitrust laws that first saw the light of day in 1890 should be applied to the super-modern, high-tech industries of the 21st century. But it is precisely these 'high-tech' industries, based on intellectual capital, to which competition law should be applied with the greatest force, not only in America, but in Britain – perhaps especially in Britain, where the entrepreneurial spirit is just beginning to push its way through the historic barriers to risk-taking and daring.

The so-called high-tech industries – and I use the term 'so-called' because I am not certain just which industries to include and which to exclude from that category (are the robot-driven assembly lines of the auto industry and the highly computerised steel manufacturing process high or low tech?) – are driven by pizza-eating, very young, ill-dressed entrepreneurs. These entrepreneurs, some of them due to become billionaires or mere millionaires, others running out of cash or due to do so very soon, often threaten the very existence of incumbent firms – not just a bit of their market share, but their very survival. If those incumbent firms have substantial market power, they can crush the new entrants unless they are barred from using a variety of tactics that artificially raise barriers to entry.

This is, of course, true in all industries. But more so in the case of high-tech start-ups. In these industries we rely on waves of creatively destructive innovation to be the principal engines of progress. In many of these industries, newcomers rely on venture capitalists for the seed capital needed to take their idea from concept to marketable product. These venture capitalists are notably hard-headed realists. If they believe that an entrenched incumbent will be allowed to snuff out incipient competition by inducing manufacturers to boycott the new product, or by using pricing schemes that make it uneconomic for manufacturers of hardware to adopt new software, or by using technological legerdemain to tie its own competing product to its monopoly product, venture capitalists will suggest to the newcomer that completion of his doctoral dissertation or a job with the entrenched incumbent is his best option.

So it is important to keep the flow of innovations coming, and to make sure that powerful incumbents cannot erect artificial roadblocks to their introduction and diffusion. To do that will require not only that cases be brought when threats to the competitive process emerge, but that remedies be fashioned that are effective.

That is why the Department of Justice has it right in seeking structural relief – divestiture – in the Microsoft case.

Given the business practices of Microsoft, which were nothing more modern or high-tech than tying the availability of a monopoly product to the customer's willingness to use the Microsoft entry in more competitive markets, Judge Jackson didn't have to make new law to find that Microsoft was in violation of the antitrust laws.

But what to do about it? If the government attempted to fashion a remedy that regulates Microsoft's future business conduct, it would find itself in the impossible position of reviewing technological advances, deciding what should and what should not be incorporated in the operating system, and which of Microsoft's future contractual terms went beyond commercial necessity and became instruments for stifling competition. That would mean having the court sit in judgement for years to come on the details of Microsoft's daily operating decisions. No court is competent to do that: the pace of innovation would be slowed, and competitors of Microsoft would forever be petitioning the judge to stop Microsoft from doing first this and then that.

In short, an efficient remedy in the case of a high-tech violator of the antitrust laws cannot require on-going judicial supervision of the practices of a company specialising in the creation of intellectual property, for the obvious reason that we do not want to slow the breakneck pace of innovation to accommodate the more leisurely one of the judicial process. This means that relief will have to be more radical in the case of high-tech violators of the antitrust laws than in the case of lower-tech ones, with divestiture and structural solutions playing a larger role relative to the prohibition of specific practices.*

5. *People matter.* It is blindingly obvious to those of us who are involved in the application of competition law that no legislation is better than those charged with its enforcement. As George Yarrow has pointed out, 'A high burden of responsibility will . . . fall upon the enforcement agencies.'

This is a semi-polite way of saying that a major upgrading of the economic skills of the various bodies charged with the enforcement of the competition laws is badly needed. This is not a game for the amateur, no matter how gifted. It is a game for the economically literate, which category need not be restricted to professional economists.

Nor is it a macho game, in which a highly visible competition cop takes on an equally visible corporate chieftain, to the delight of the media and politicians. One of Microsoft's many mistakes was to personalise its antitrust case by gambling that Bill Gates's nerdy looks and soft-sell personality would trump the reality of his distinctly un-nerdy and hard-line behaviour as reflected in his e-mails and his company's practices.

And one of the early problems Britain faced in regulating its newly privatised industries was the tendency of some regulators and some CEOs to personalise the regulatory process, rather than to view it as an impersonal process of the application of law to business behaviour.

---

* The trial court has ordered divestiture. That decision is on appeal.

Which is why the Secretary of State for Trade and Industry has it right when he attempts to 'depersonalise' the enforcement process.

But because the quality of the enforcement authorities importantly influences the effectiveness of competition policy, there is more to be done than 'depersonalisation'. Those toiling at the enforcement agencies would, I am sure, welcome a systematic programme to better acquaint them with the latest economic thinking as to market definition, the measurement of monopoly profits, the tools for separating predatory from merely tough competition, and the host of other concepts that are constantly being re-examined and refined by academic economists.*

Surely, working seminars sponsored by the OFT and other agencies, and by outside organisations such as the IEA, would be useful supplements to the internal training programmes of the OFT, for example, as Britain struggles to match the competence of its enforcement agencies with the magnitude of the task they face.

---

* Such a programme is now in operation, as mentioned in the lecture immediately following this one.

Competition policy and superior macroeconomic performance: you can't have one without the other

The following lecture was delivered on 15 November 2000 at No. 11 Downing Street under the auspices of the Adam Smith Institute and at the request of Chancellor of the Exchequer Gordon Brown. It explores the relationship between competition policy and such macroeconomic indicators of performance as productivity growth, economic growth and the diffusion of economic opportunity.

It is a great pleasure to be with you this morning; I admire the willingness of people in this country to attend breakfast-time conferences and hope that this barbaric practice doesn't spread to my more relaxed country.

This might seem to be an odd venue in which to be having a discussion of competition policy. Traditionally, there has been a clear separation between macroeconomic policy, considered the purview of the Treasury, and microeconomic policy, to be left to the Department of Trade and Industry and a variety of enforcement agencies. The Treasury would see to fiscal and monetary policy, the big picture, and leave to others the problem of working out a policy that would create competition, if indeed such a policy were deemed desirable – a view not unanimously held in the business community or in ministries that see their role as sponsoring a variety of national champions.

Thanks to the efforts of the Chancellor, this gap between macroeconomic and microeconomic policy is now being bridged. The motives for constructing this bridge are clear: long-term growth in productivity is a necessity if the economy is to grow without significant inflation, if living standards are to rise, and if the Treasury's coffers are to bulge. Also, the programmes of a centre-left government require money to pay for them. And it is increasingly clear that governments of all political stripes are reaching the outer limits of their ability to extract from their citizens a larger portion of their hard-earned money – at least, they are reaching the limits of their ability to do so overtly. It is deemed by all save a very few to be politically impossible to raise income taxes openly; and recent events [this was a reference to the protests over high petrol taxes, which protests disrupted transport, food deliveries and the lives of commuters] suggest that indirect taxes are increasingly unpopular, and difficult to conceal from notice.

To the political difficulties add the economic fact that capital and labour are increasingly mobile and willing to migrate to more hospitable climes from jurisdictions in which taxes have become vexatious.

So any government of the centre-left, interested in expanding the role of government, either by spending more on existing programmes in the hope that greater inputs will translate into greater outputs (a hope not borne out by experience), or by initiating new programmes, must rely on economic growth to throw off the huge sums of taxes that might at least partially satisfy the appetite of its Treasury for an ever-increasing portion of the nation's GDP – one is reminded of Queen Gertrude, whose appetite for the charms of King Hamlet increased 'by what it fed on'!

This growth can be generated in two ways. More people can be put to work turning out goods and services, and the productivity of the workforce can be increased. This government is attempting to increase the workforce by a number of measures designed to make work more attractive than malingering, increase the training of those with too few skills to participate in the workforce, maintain a stable economic environment, and, of late, by relaxing some of its restrictions on immigration.

And it has emphasised the need to increase productivity. Just last week the Chancellor repeated his plea to what I believe are called your 'European partners' to reform their economies so that they might 'achieve what I believe is now the prize within our grasp – US levels of productivity and thus long-term prosperity for all'. This is not the place to share with you my views on the level of enthusiasm in some European countries for the reforms the Chancellor quite correctly advocates, or on the likelihood that the French and some other 'partners' will rally to the call to be more like Americans. But it is the place to comment on the key role of a vigorous competition policy in achieving, here in Britain, the rapid, inflation-free economic growth that, in the end, will add more to the wealth of the nation and welfare of its citizens than all of the redistribution schemes combined. A larger and larger economic pie is likely to prove more satisfying than thinner and thinner slices of one of fixed size.

Which is one reason why the Chancellor has been so keen to couple his redistribution programme with one that raises the UK trend growth rate by increasing productivity.[82] There is, of course, a danger when governments take an interest in microeconomic policy: they tend to tinker in the belief that a bit of taxation here, a bit of tax relief there, a subsidy or two, regulatory intervention,

---

82 It is not clear just how well Britain is doing in comparison with other countries. According to a recent Treasury report ('Productivity in the UK: The Evidence and the Government's Approach', November 2000), 'Whichever measure of productivity is used . . . the UK has a sizeable gap compared with other major industrialised countries' (p. 6). But a recent study by Goldman Sachs takes a cheerier view of UK experience and of the magnitude of information and communications technology (ICT) investment. See that firm's 'The IT Revolution – New Data on the Global Impact', October 2000.

some exhortation, and none-too-subtle pressure on business leaders can produce the productivity gains they seek, in the places they think most important.

Such programmes are generally counterproductive. Not so a vigorous competition policy, which has certain advantages that are worth rehearsing briefly:

1. A policy that makes it difficult for businessmen to collude to fix prices guarantees consumers that the prices they pay for goods and services will reflect only the costs of producing the goods and services they buy, including a reasonable return on the capital committed to the production of those goods and services. As Alfred Marshall long ago stated, in the days when the economic literature consisted of clear, equation-free prose, 'If the producers of a commodity are many in number and act without any concert, it is to the interest of each of them to increase his supply of it whenever he expects to obtain a price greater than its Expenses of production. So that the price of a commodity cannot long exceed its Expenses of production, if there is free competition among its producers.'[83]

2. A concomitant result of an effective competition policy is that competing businesses will be under pressure to produce in the most efficient manner – minimising costs so that they are in a position to meet or beat the prices of their competitors. This of course is one reason why competition policy has not been uniformly popular in Britain: it discourages

---

83 Alfred and Mary Paley Marshall, *The Economics of Industry*, Thoemmes Press, Bristol, 1994, reprinting the original 1879 edition, p. 180.

overmanning, and runs counter to several government policies such as that designed to preserve jobs in the coal industry by preventing the construction of gas-fired power stations. In short, if efficiency and high productivity are your goals, competition policy is for you; if preserving jobs at the expense of efficiency is what you prefer, it (rather like free trade) is not for you.

3. A vigorous competition policy should maximise the rate of innovation and the rate of introduction of new technologies, in the process denying what Hicks identified as the greatest monopoly profit – a quiet life.[84] I recognise that the economic literature on this point is ambiguous, since it recognises the possibility that competition in product markets might deny innovators the ability to appropriate to themselves the fruits of their inventions, thereby discouraging expenditure on research and development.[85] But here I would like to draw on John Vickers' formulation, offered in a paper considering the relation between competition and productive efficiency: 'Competition seems very well in practice, but it is not so clear how it works in theory.'[86] For a commonsense appraisal of real-life experience – the comparison of efficiency in countries with and without competitive market systems; Microsoft's efforts to deny innovators access to markets and the effect that had on potential competitors' access to venture capital; the rapid introduction of new electric generating technologies when competition was opened up in the electricity market;

---

84 J. R. Hicks, *Value and Capital*, Clarendon Press, Oxford, 1939.

85 In this connection see Donald Hay and John Vickers (eds), *The Economics of Market Dominance*, Basil Blackwell, Oxford, 1986, pp. 8–9.

86 John Vickers, 'Concepts of Competition', *Oxford Economic Papers* 47, 1995, p. 1.

the innovative services offered by the airline industry when competition replaced regulation – suggests to me that competition means a fiercer gale of creative destruction than does the cosier world of cartels and monopoly.

This is especially important in this age of the Internet and related technologies. I recognise that the claims for this technology are somewhat overblown, and that electricity, the telephone, the automobile and perhaps other inventions can claim to have had a greater impact. No matter: we are in the midst of what Schumpeter referred to as a 'cluster'. Some 65 years ago Schumpeter wrote, 'Why should the carrying into effect of innovations . . . *cluster* at certain times . . . ? One answer suggests itself immediately: as soon as the various kinds of social resistance to something that is fundamentally new and untried have been overcome, it is much easier not to do the same thing again . . . so that a first success will always produce a cluster . . . This is indeed the method of *competitive capitalism* . . .'[87]

If we are indeed entering into or are in the early stages of a 'cluster' of innovation, we should be especially alert to efforts by those threatened by change to deploy anti-competitive weapons in order to thwart the diffusion of new inventions and techniques.

4. A vigorous competition policy also provides a tool with which to judge which mergers are in the public interest, and which are not. The dividing line is simple to describe, if not always

---

87 Joseph A. Schumpeter, 'The Analysis of Economic Change', *Review of Economic Statistics*, May 1935, reprinted in Richard V. Clemence (ed.), *Essays on Entrepreneurial Innovations, Business Cycles, and the Evolution of Capitalism*, Transaction Publishers, New Brunswick, New Jersey, 1989, pp. 141–2.

easy to discern: any merger that unduly reduces competition or threatens to do so should be halted. Note: it is not necessary for the minister to decide whether he thinks the merger is a good idea, and is likely to produce the anticipated savings (most do not). Nor is it for him to decide how many football fans might be offended, and how many pleased; or how a specific marginal constituency might react; or whether he regards the executives and boards of the acquiring companies as good chaps. All he need do is satisfy himself that he has so structured, funded and staffed the relevant competition authority that it is competent to appraise the competitive impact of mergers. Issues of national defence, of course, might be an exception, although I have never seen proof that a nation's defence effort is enhanced by forcing the military authorities to purchase in non-competitive markets.

5. Effective competition makes regulation unnecessary. It is important to distinguish competition policy from regulatory policy. Some industries contain significant natural monopoly elements, and therefore must have their prices, performance and profits regulated lest they exploit their customers. In other industries, competition is possible but can be snuffed out or seriously diluted by the exercise of market power that in no sense flows 'naturally' from the economic structure of the industry. By preventing the untoward exercise of market power, the competition authorities preserve the market's ability to determine prices and allocate resources, making regulation unnecessary. In short, *ad hoc* interventions to preserve competition make on-going regulation unnecessary, for where the invisible hand operates, the heavy hand of government is not necessary to assure consumers against exploitation.

6. Finally, a proper competition policy produces a variety of desirable social effects – the diffusion of economic power and the maximisation of economic and social mobility. In an economy in which incumbent firms cannot create artificial barriers to entry, either by deploying their own market power or by colluding with others, fledgling entrepreneurs are likely to flourish. This is important not only to maintaining a high rate of invention and innovation – competitive entry, after all, inevitably destroys the value of existing investments – but to maintaining a society that is deemed to be fair and open by its citizens.[88] In America, the relative ease of entry has contributed to the mobility among income groups that has prevented the class warfare so common in other countries. Note, however, that it is precisely this result of competition policy that generates opposition to it by those in government who prefer to manage the rate of change in society, by those classes that prefer the status quo to a society in which *arrivistes* can eventually despoil the neighbourhoods of those with 'old money' by moving there, and by businessmen with undepreciated sunk investment that will never be recovered if barriers to entry are eliminated.

Let me turn now to the ingredients of a successful competition policy. They are three.

First, the legislation mandating it must be properly drawn. Second, the agency or agencies established to enforce that policy must be staffed with able men and women: economically literate,

---

88   In this connection see Shenefield and Stelzer, op. cit., pp. 10–14. See also Stephen Martin, *Industrial Economics: Economic Analysis and Public Policy*, Prentice Hall, Englewood Cliffs, New Jersey, 1994, pp. 45–50.

free of biases against business in general and big business in particular, and independent of the politicians who appoint them. Third, the procedures followed by these agencies must be conducive to ascertaining all of the facts and competing interpretations of those facts that a conscientious agency staff and director need in order to reach considered judgements on very difficult issues.

Let me treat each of those in turn:

1. *Legislation*: In Britain, the legislation now embodying the competitive rules of the game is likely to be significantly more effective than was the old regime. But that new legislation nevertheless is seriously flawed. Those businessmen who decide whether to compete or collude, and whether to compete fairly or abuse their market power, have all to gain and little to lose by violating the law. True, there is the possibility of financial penalties equal to 10 per cent of UK group turnover for up to three years if the infringement lasted for at least that period. But fines are paid by the shareholders, not by the executives who concocted the anti-competitive schemes. And unless you believe that the same executives who blithely decouple their compensation from their success in building value for their shareholders worry excessively about mere fines, which they will not pay from personal resources, you must agree that fines may not be a serious deterrent to anti-competitive behaviour.

I agree, of course, that fines, the leniency[89] now offered to 'whistle-blowers', and threats of irritating and unsettling 'dawn

---

89 This leniency policy, modelled on that of the US Department of Justice, is offered to undertakings that are the first to come forward before an investigation has commenced and before the OFT has sufficient evidence to establish the existence

raids' will have some effect on the propensity of business executives to fix prices and otherwise undermine market forces. But in the case of price-fixing conspiracies, big fines are a less effective deterrent than small jail sentences. In America, it is the threat of a stretch as a guest of the government that keeps many an executive out of a smoke-filled room (actually, price fixers probably now meet in the smoke-free environments of various hotel suites) in which prices can be discussed and co-ordinated, as John Shenefield, formerly head of the antitrust division, pointed out to me earlier this week.

Britain has no such deterrent, which is doubly surprising now that your Home Secretary has decided that miscreants should be jailed only by day, and then let loose at night. Just as this will free garden-variety crooks such as burglars and muggers to pursue their trade after a day's rest and three square meals at the government's expense, so would this regime leave executives jailed for price fixing free to complete their social and dinner commitments.

Seriously, I believe you will find that it will be a long while before mere fines will destroy the culture of price fixing that permeates British business.

And I doubt, too, that the threat of damage suits, as provided for in the new Act, will be an effective deterrent. True, an injured party can bring a suit to recover damages. These suits are expensive, and the 'loser pays' doctrine is likely to deter all save the best-financed firms from pursuing this remedy. The larger,

---

of the alleged cartel; that provide complete information and on-going co-operation; that did not instigate the cartel activities or coerce others into joining the cartel; and that quit the cartel after informing on it. See 'Director-General of Fair Trading's Guidance as to the Appropriate Amount of a Penalty', Office of Fair Trading, March 2000, pp. 6–8.

better-financed firms, of course, are more likely to be members of the 'club', and therefore less likely to attack their golfing partners in court.

Even if a plaintiff does prevail, the miscreant pays back his ill-gotten gains – and no more. Given that the probability of being sued is less than one, and that the probability that the complainant will prevail is also less than one, it pays for a potential conspirator or monopolist to chance paying such damages – nothing to lose, and all to gain. In America, of course, damages are trebled, so that a violator of the law must reckon that he may indeed lose a great deal if he is found to have illegally injured a competitor.

2. *Staffing*: There are two aspects to staffing: quantity and quality. Since even the best of economists, lawyers, accountants and other professionals cannot do good work if overtaxed (a phrase I use with some trepidation in this venue!), it is good that the staffs of the various agencies are being expanded. Even a conservative (small 'c') such as I, who believes that that government is best which governs least, recognises that a more vibrant competition policy warrants the expansion of the Competition Policy Division now under way.[90] Good competition policy cannot be bought on the cheap, and pays for itself many times over.

Then there is the question of quality. Constitutionalists are fond of saying that yours is a government of laws, not men. They make the same point in my country. Even a brief descent from the

---

90 That division 'now has approaching 170 staff and is still expanding. We have recruited 55 new members of staff, mostly lawyers and economists . . . ' Margaret Bloom, 'The New UK Competition Act', speech to the 27th International Antitrust Law & Policy Conference, Fordham University, New York City, 19 October 2000.

ivory tower, however, introduces those of us who work in the competition policy field to the reality that the quality of mind and the views of the men and women charged with enforcing the competition laws have a major effect on the effectiveness of those laws.

Start with ministers: some believe that cases should rise or fall on the single question of the effect of the questioned practice or merger on competition; others posit broader 'public interest' goals, such as the effect on jobs, or the relative economic health of regions (by which I believe they mean constituencies). To the extent that competitive criteria are more susceptible of definition and measurement than is the concept of the public interest, reliance on those economic criteria is more likely to produce consistency and certainty, and less likely to produce political lobbying, than is the introduction of a public interest test. So my own preference is for a policy that relies solely on economic criteria.

But before you say, 'He would, wouldn't he; after all he is an economist', let me add one thought. I am fully aware that economics is not a value-free discipline. When we say that we prefer competition to regulation, we are saying that we are elevating the interests of consumers over other, competing interests; when we say that prices and the allocation of goods, services and resources are best left to the market, we are assuming that the current distribution of income is in some sense 'fair', or at least fairer, and incomes certainly higher, than they would be if politicians replaced markets as the allocators of the nation's resources. We would add that it is more efficient for societies dissatisfied with the way income is distributed, or the balance that competition produces between consumer and producer interests, to make the desired adjustments directly, by direct subsidies and income transfers, than it is to distort markets. In short: better to pay a fuel allowance than to distort electricity and gas markets by mandating artificially low prices; better to arrange direct income transfers if a region is adversely affected by a merger that does not substantially reduce competition, than to prevent the merger.

So one must applaud the efforts of the Secretary of State for Trade and Industry to extricate himself from the process of deciding which mergers may go forward, and which may not. That should leave the competition issues with the competition authorities. If politicians then wish to inject considerations other than competitive impact into the mix to counter or modify the results of a decision, they have the legislative tools to do so.

Ministers, of course, also play a role in the selection of those who direct the enforcement of competition policy. This group includes members of the Competition Commission; the Director-General of the Office of Fair Trading; the sector regulators;[91] and the boards that will soon be named to advise the various directors-general on the policies of their respective agencies. As I have pointed out elsewhere,[92] Britain has been extraordinarily fortunate in its staffing of these important posts – not uniformly fortunate, of course, but in general quite well served.

And there is no question that two relatively recent developments will improve the quality of enforcement. The first is the training programme instituted by the Office of Fair Trading in May of last year to educate its staff and the staffs of the sector reg-

---

91 Gas and electricity, OFGEM; telecommunications, OFTEL; water services, OFWAT; Office for the Regulation of Electricity and Gas (Northern Ireland), OFREG; and the Rail Regulator, ORR.

92 'A Review of Privatisation and Regulation Experience in Britain', the Beesley Lectures on Regulation, London, 7 November 2000 (see pp. 144–65 of this volume).

ulators in the law and economics of competition policy.[93] The second is the increased reliance on the best sorts of people to enforce competition laws – economists. Since the alternative is usually a lawyer, I am doubly relieved to see that policy is in the hands of economists. After all, lawyers' devotion to competition is somewhat diluted by the anti-competitive practices they have found so useful in imposing on society their own view of the proper distribution of the nation's income. I find it wholly appropriate that an agency headed by an economist will be carrying out the Secretary of Trade and Industry's request 'to undertake a review of restrictions on competition in the professions, including restrictions on entry to a profession, reserving categories of work to certain professions, and advertising'.[94]

My hope is that the increasing economic sophistication of this generation of decision-makers – and I mean no offence to their predecessors such as Sir Bryan Carsberg who, although afflicted with an accountant's training, somehow managed to rise above it and think like an economist – will bring greater clarity to questions such as the definition of relevant markets and the distinction between competitive and anti-competitive behaviour.

These are difficult questions, to be sure. As Donald Hay and Derek Morris point out, 'There are rather few examples of market structure or conduct which we can condemn unambiguously as not being in the public interest. Similarly, there are few market practices to which we can give a definitive assent. In most examples, "it all depends" on the particular circumstances under consideration

---

[93] 'Annual Report of the Director-General of Fair Trading to the Secretary of State for Trade and Industry', January–December 1999, p. 40.

[94] Rt Hon. Stephen Byers, 'Consumers and Competitive Markets', speech at the Social Market Foundation, London, 21 September 2000, p. 4 (mimeo).

... The investigation of the particular circumstances will be no easy task.'[95] It is not easy to determine the outer limits of a product market – which products limit the pricing discretion available to producers of other products. Nor is it easy to determine whether a firm has achieved a dominant position, 'as a consequence of a superior product, business acumen, or historic accident',[96] to which sound competition policy does not object, or by the use of anti-competitive tactics. Nor is it easy to distinguish predatory behaviour from the normal competitive give-and-take one hopes will animate rivals in their efforts to attract and retain consumers.

But I think it not unfair to say that the market definitions chosen have too often been driven by the results sought, rather than by rigorous analysis, and conclusions concerning the propriety of competitive tactics too often reflect a desire to conclude an investigation with a self-applauding press release, rather than an effort to construct a coherent analysis of the real facts prevailing in the marketplace.

These missteps can be made less frequent by an improvement in procedures, to which I now turn.

3. *Procedure*: Here, there is considerable room for improvement. My own experience is that the procedures used in arriving at decisions could benefit from the introduction of more adversarial techniques. I am aware, of course, that the nature of the relationship between a firm being investigated and the investigating agency is quite adversarial. But the method of gathering evidence

---

95 Donald A. Hay and Derek J. Morris, *Industrial Economics and Organization: Theory and Evidence*, Oxford University Press, Oxford, 1991, p. 609.

96 *United States* v. *Grinnell Corp.*, 384 US 563 (1966).

and expert opinion is not. The OFT will tell a firm under investigation that it has received complaints from unnamed parties about certain behaviour, but will not make the complaint and its supporting evidence available. Experts will appear before the Competition Commission, offer differing interpretations of the facts, but never be required to confront one another so that a discussion of the differences can reveal to decision-makers the strengths and weaknesses of each position. The staffs of the agencies are not required to undergo cross-examination by private parties in the presence of their directors-general so that these directors-general can fully appraise and understand the quality of the advice they are being given; instead they generally rely on the staff's version of the other party's contentions.

As I said earlier, the issues in these cases are extraordinarily difficult, once we get beyond cases of overt price fixing, replete with smoking guns. The quality of decisions can only benefit from a full vetting of the facts and analysis underlying the contentions of the opposing parties.

And the consistency of policy can only benefit from a reduction in the opaqueness that often characterises decisions. These documents are extremely important, not only because they resolve the case at issue, one way or the other, but because if well drafted they provide businessmen and their counsel with a guide to future behaviour.

Let me now turn to a question that is increasingly raised: Should traditional competition policy be applied to the new, so-called high-tech industries? The short answer is 'yes'[97] [for reasons

---

97   In this connection see Edward D. Cavanagh, 'Antitrust Remedies in Monopolization Cases: A Look Back and a Look Ahead', delivered at the American Bar Association Antitrust Section, 11 July 2000. Cavanagh, Professor of Law at St John's

set forth in my lecture to the Federalist Society, reprinted herein].

I would like to close on this final note. Thanks to the Chancellor, we are witnessing a recognition of the fact that competition policy has an important role to play in achieving the macroeconomic goal of sustained non-inflationary economic growth. We now look at this aspect of microeconomic policy through the prism of the goals of macroeconomic policy. But we must also do the obverse, and recognise that macroeconomic policy, and most notably taxation, must not inhibit our ability to achieve the microeconomic goals of greater entrepreneurship, efficiency and productivity. High and rising taxes on what to left-leaning politicians seem like 'high earners', limitations on share option schemes, tax regimes so complex that no small businessman can hope to cope with them, taxes that discourage the lone entrepreneur working from his home – all of these offset the beneficial effects of a vigorous competition policy. If microeconomic policy is to be put to the service of macroeconomic policy, macroeconomic policy must not be so crafted as to offset the gains that vigorous competition policy can bring.

University, argues that the presence of network externalities may create antitrust problems in high-tech markets, and that the argument that high-tech markets are self-correcting 'is to a great extent just old wine in new bottles'. See also *The Economist*, 6 March 1999, pp. 21–2.

2 THOUGHTS ON REGULATORY POLICY

Lessons for UK regulation from recent US experience

This lecture was delivered at the Royal Society of Arts, London, on 7 December 1995 as part of a series of lectures on regulatory policy sponsored by the Institute of Economic Affairs. * *By this time I had overcome my reluctance to hold American experience up as a model from which British policy-makers might have something to learn. It is satisfying to note that British regulatory policy has recently moved in the direction of American policy, especially in the matter of procedure, with single regulators now benefiting from advisory boards, and the process of decision-making becoming more transparent.*

I have three reasons for approaching the assignment of concluding this most distinguished lecture series with great trepidation. First, it is daunting to follow so distinguished a group of speakers, all of whom were able to enrich the knowledge of an audience already as well informed as this one. Second, it is somewhat awkward for an American to appear before a British audience to suggest ways in which its members might improve – by being more like Americans! Third, my assignment is fraught with peril. I am asked to

---

*   Subsequently published in M. E. Beesley (ed.), *Regulating Utilities: A Time for Change?*, Readings 44, Institute of Economic Affairs, London, 1996.

extract from recent American experience with regulation some 'Lessons for UK Regulation'. This assignment rests on two rather dubious assumptions:

1. It assumes that a foreigner can understand just what is going on in Britain's regulatory arena. That is an heroic assumption, since the regulatory process here is not as transparent as the one in my country, a point to which I shall return in a moment. In his wonderful book on your country's constitution, Peter Hennessy refers to '... this curious compound of custom and precedent, law and convention, rigidity and malleability concealed beneath layers of opacity and mystery ... '[1] I won't go so far as to argue that Britain's regulatory process is as opaque and mysterious as its constitution. But I will suggest – by way of exculpation for any errors I am about to make – that an outside observer such as myself does not always find the published decisions of regulators, the competition authorities and the Department of Trade and Industry a crystal-clear guide as to what really went on, what was really decided, and what, in apparently similar circumstances, might be decided in the future.

2. A second, and even more problematic, assumption underlying my topic, 'Lessons for UK Regulation from Recent US Experience', is that it assumes that someone in Britain believes that it is indeed possible to learn from American experience. Experience teaches me, however, that an American imprimatur does not guarantee that an idea or product will be well received here. It is not the

---

1   Peter Hennessy, *The Hidden Wiring: Unearthing The British Constitution*, Victor Gollancz, London, 1995, p. 7.

equivalent of a royal warrant. Indeed, it has been my experience that my British friends very often succeed in scuppering an idea they find disagreeable by the simple expedient of labelling it 'American-style', as in the phrase 'American-style fast food'. Thus, when the debate about aviation policy was raging here, anyone who suggested that American experience with free and open competition might contain lessons for Britain was accused of proposing 'American-style deregulation', code words for anarchy and chaos. And when the various 'OFFs' – wat, gas, er and tel – were being established, any suggestion that procedures be adopted to make the regulatory process transparent and accessible to all affected parties was derided as an invitation to 'American-style litigation', a fate that would eventually doom regulators to be harassed by (a) silly consumers who presumed to know when they were receiving poor service and when they were being held to ransom, and (b) potential new entrants who thought that a willingness to risk their capital somehow gave them the right to compete with incumbent service providers.

True, 'the litigious nature of the American [cost-plus] system ... might have posed less acute problems in the more secretive British framework', as one leading British academic has argued.[2] But it was, nevertheless, to be avoided. (I am not here arguing in favour of a full-employment act for lawyers. Or even for economists, although such legislation would have one major advantage: economists involved in regulatory proceedings would have less time to unburden themselves of economic forecasts.)

Indeed, so great was and is the fear of 'American-style litiga-

---

2   Catherine Price, 'Economic Regulation of Privatised Monopolies', in Peter M. Jackson and Catherine M. Price, *Privatisation and Regulation: A Review of the Issues*, Longman Group Ltd, 1994, p. 82.

tion' that one would think that acceptance of the American procedural model would doom Britain to a situation in which it would be impossible for ambulance drivers to respond to emergency calls lest they run down the horde of fee-crazed lawyers that would be spawned as the American disease spread from the offices of the regulatory bodies onto the streets of Britain's cities and towns like some noxious plague.

This decision to establish a decision-making process that, to all intents and purposes, excluded consumers from participation relied on the very English notion that responsible chaps know what is best for the public. So the government established a regime in which the director-general of this or that 'OFF' would sit down with his counterpart in the regulated company and come to a mutually agreeable determination of just where the public interest lies.

This had – and still has – two serious drawbacks. First, it severely limits the range of inputs available to the regulator. Second, it denies to the regulators' decisions the credibility that only open systems can provide.

Another error was to rely on a single decision-maker, the director-general. This tends to personalise the regulatory process, producing a stream of 'look what Bryan Carsberg has done now in his mad effort to inject competition'; 'how could Professor Littlechild be so unworldly as to suggest he might review regulatory policy when such a review might move markets'; 'look how much Ms Spottiswoode is being paid'; and 'why is Don Cruickshank trying to wreck BT?' A good example of this personalisation is reflected in a recent report on page one of the *Financial Times* (24 November 1995): 'the war of words' between Don Cruickshank, Director-General of Oftel, and Sir Ian Vallance, Chairman of BT, said the paper, escalated as Sir Ian wondered 'what lies behind the director-general's ambitions' and Mr Cruickshank questioned BT's business ethics. Policy becomes obscured by personality.

This personalisation of the regulatory process might have been avoided had the government looked to US experience and chosen one of the two alternative regulatory formats available to it. It could have set up multi-member commissions to monitor each of the regulated industries, or it could have established a single, multi-member regulatory body to monitor them all. Consider, for a moment, the advantages of the latter structure, one which is used in almost all states in America.

The problems facing regulators in the gas, electric and telecoms industries have much in common – water, I believe, may be a special case. Each of these industries is regulated so that the prices it charges change in line with the Retail Price Index (RPI) minus some X factor to account for productivity improvements. Initially, X was of necessity set quite arbitrarily. As Professors Beesley and Littlechild so elegantly put it, 'There is nothing unique, optimal, or mechanical about the initial choice of X.'[3] After all, who could tell just how much fat had accumulated on the bones of the publicly owned utilities during their long, slothful period of inactivity in the public sector? And who could tell just how much improvement in productivity it would be possible to obtain?

But as time passed, the staffs of the regulatory agencies should have been able to move to more reasoned determinations of X. They became familiar with various studies of total factor productivity, and of the advantages and limits of using benchmarks,

3   M. E. Beesley and S. C. Littlechild, 'The Regulation of Privatised Monopolies in the United Kingdom', in Cento Veljanovski (ed.), *Regulators and the Market*, Institute of Economic Affairs, London, 1991, p. 38.

perhaps even benchmarks derived from international data of the sort recently used by Oftel to raise questions about BT's efficiency. The underlying techniques involved in doing such productivity studies are quite the same, whether one is dealing with the electric industry, the gas industry or the telecoms industry. Surely there must be advantages to having one regulatory body perform these analyses for all of the regulated industries?

So, too, with questions of access. The competition policy and other economic issues involved in determining the terms of access to the telecoms, gas and electric networks are certainly not identical. But they have sufficient similarities so that there are economies of scale in the process of learning how to deal with them – a regulator who has confronted the problem in one industry has moved up the learning curve sufficiently to have a head start when he confronts it in another.

In the event, the government decided that the American procedural model – open hearings, multi-member regulatory bodies, an overall OFREG, instead of OFTEL, OFGAS and OFFER* – was not to be adopted in Britain. It decided, too, that the American method of setting prices on the basis of cost-plus-a-reasonable-return was not acceptable, and that it was preferable to develop a system in which the prices charged by the newly privatised utilities would be related to the rate of inflation with adjustments for projected improvements in productivity. The reasons for rejecting use of cost-of-service regulation were two: a fear that cost-plus pricing provides no incentive to efficient operations, and a feeling that the 'plus', i.e. the cost of capital, could not be determined with acceptable precision.

---

*   Since this lecture was delivered, the originally separate gas and electricity regulatory agencies have been merged, and plans are afoot to merge the various agencies involved in the regulation of the various telecoms and media industries.

The first of these fears has some basis in fact – but only some. For it gives no weight to what is known as 'regulatory lag'. Outside observers see the sometimes leisurely pace of America's regulatory proceedings as an unambiguous evil. They miss an important point: regulatory lag provides the incentive to efficient operation that would be absent were cost-of-service regulation instantaneous. For regulated companies know that if they succeed in lowering their costs it will be some time before the regulator will initiate hearings, and even longer before he concludes them. During that time, the increased profits resulting from the lower costs will flow through to the bottom line and to the shareholder. Similarly, if the companies allow costs to rise, it may be some time before the procedure for obtaining relief is concluded, during which time profits will fall.

Thus does regulatory lag provide an incentive to efficiency that would otherwise be absent from a cost-based regulatory system. In short, cost-of-service regulation provides some of the advantages that British policy-makers thought inhered only in the RPI-X formula. And it avoids the problem created by a lack of explicit attention to the possibility of monopoly profits.

The second factor that led to the rejection of a cost-based regulatory scheme was the perception that it would be difficult to determine the rate of return investors should be allowed to earn on the capital prudently committed to the business. That important conceptual and data problems face anyone charged with the responsibility for determining what is known as a fair rate of return there can be no question, as both Alfred Kahn[4] in my country, and

---

4   Alfred E. Kahn, *The Economics of Regulation: Principles and Institutions*, vol. 1, John Wiley & Sons, Inc., New York, 1970, pp. 45–54.

John Vickers in yours, have pointed out, the latter calling profit measures 'subjective, open to manipulation, and prone to an inherent problem of circularity'.[5] But neither can there be any question that the theoretical and data problems facing anyone attempting to determine the appropriate rate of anticipated productivity improvement, X, make those faced by a seeker after the cost of capital, k, seem trivial by comparison. In part this is because the resources-rich financial community has long had a stake in sharpening the analytical tools with which to measure the cost of capital and such of its components as the financial and other risks faced by investors. In part, too, it is due to the fact that generations of regulatory hearings in the United States have invited those with different theories of cost-of-capital measurement to thrash out their differences, while efforts to measure such concepts as total factor productivity are a relatively new element of regulatory proceedings.

But there is a more fundamental and enduring reason why it will always be more problematic to determine X than k. There are real transactions involving real money in real, competitive financial markets to guide us towards at least reasonable approximations of what any regulated firm must pay to attract capital. But when we turn to X we set sail on a sea of doubt. We are trying to capture the cost reductions that would have occurred naturally, as the result of exogenous forces and the intrinsic character of the industry under examination, and without any particularly distinguished management effort. That natural or automatic portion of any improvement in productivity will go to customers in the form

---

5   Colin Mayer and John Vickers, 'Profit-sharing Regulation – An Economic Appraisal', September 1995, p. 11 (mimeo).

of lower prices. (I leave aside, as requiring a separate paper, the question of which customers should be selected by the regulator as beneficiaries of this natural rate of productivity improvement.) Any productivity gain in excess of the natural rate is assumed – and I do mean assumed – to be attributable to some extraordinary skill and effort on the part of management, and therefore flows through to shareholders – after, of course, the managers appropriate a modest portion for themselves by way of self-congratulation.

Unfortunately for the British consumer, it was impossible for anyone in authority to imagine just how inefficient the public sector utilities had become. As John Reynolds, electricity analyst with James Capel, has pointed out, '... everyone underestimated the inefficiency of nationalised industry'.[6] That is not surprising, since the wild overmanning, egregious insensitivity to consumer wants, and inflated prices had all occurred under the supposedly watchful eyes of the very ministers who were now setting up the regulatory system under which X would be determined; they could hardly be expected to recognise the full extent of the inefficiencies accumulated on their watch. Of course, it was conceded, the monopoly electric service had chosen a capital-wasting means of generating electricity; true, the chaps at British Telecom had taken on rather too many staff; and there could be no denying that the management of British Gas so intimidated ministers that they dared not question the gas monopoly-monopsonist's decisions. But these minor excesses would surely disappear as the newly liberated managers pursued the incentives provided by that wondrous regulatory tool, RPI-X.

Or so everyone thought. In fact, the public sector companies

---

6   *Financial Mail on Sunday*, 26 November 1995, p. 2.

were so bloated, so inefficient, so unconcerned with that annoying creature, the customer, that it was what teenagers now call a 'no-brainer' for managers to increase efficiency at a far more rapid rate than any propounder of a specific X could imagine, with consequences I shall discuss in a moment.

Add to that the government's political calculation that Tory rule would be assured well into the next century if it could create a nation of shareholders, or at least a nation in which there were more shareholders than trade union members. This prompted it to sell off British Gas as a vertically integrated monopolist-monopsonist; to protect British Telecom from all save peripheral competition with its duopoly policy and a cable television franchising system guaranteed to prevent vigorous competition for the right to provide alternatives to BT; and to moderate the pace at which competition could be introduced into the electric supply business.

This, despite warnings and complaints from Colin Robinson,[7] George Yarrow,[8] John Vickers[9] and a host of others. I well recall

---

7   'The ... privatisation programme ... has degenerated into an exercise ... with little regard for the liberalisation of product and factor markets.' 'Privatising the Energy Industries', in Cento Veljanovski (ed.), *Privatisation & Competition: A Market Prospectus*, Institute of Economic Affairs, London, 1989, p. 113. Hereinafter, *Privatisation*.

8   '... Government policy has been distinctly less pro-competitive than would have been desirable, and regulatory policies and structures contain many weaknesses.' 'Does Ownership Matter?', in Veljanovski, *Privatisation*, p. 69.

9   'In several important respects, the regime in which BT and Mercury are to operate is by no means liberal – for example the refusal to license more public networks, and the prohibition of "resale". These are major restrictions on competition ... [T]here was no attempt to restructure BT to promote competition.' John Vickers and George Yarrow, 'Telecommunications: Liberalisation and the Privatisation of British Telecom', in John Kay, Colin Mayer and David Thompson, *Privatisation and Regulation – the UK Experience*, Clarendon Press, Oxford, 1986, p. 222.

joining Ralph Harris in a visit to the appropriate minister to plead that the gas industry be restructured before it was privatised and turned loose on an unsuspecting public. I recall, too, being told that the goals of privatisation were (1) to maximise the number of shareholders, (2) to give 'Sid' [the small shareholder] a good run for his money, and (3) to be sure not to antagonise British Gas's management. Effective regulation was notably absent from the list. All three goals were, indeed, achieved, although the last only temporarily.

These interrelated errors – closed procedures, single regulators, refusal to control profits – have now come back to haunt the government in the following ways:

1. By rejecting America's open procedural model in favour of what Professor Price calls 'the more secretive British framework', the government has denied the regulatory process the public credibility on which its success and acceptance crucially depend.
2. By rejecting the American multi-person commission in favour of a single regulator, policy-makers have personalised the regulatory process, causing issues to be fought out in the atmosphere of *High Noon*.
3. By rejecting the use of profit controls, and relying on necessarily wild and, in the event, incorrect guesses as to attainable productivity improvements, the creators of Britain's regulatory system have permitted the utilities to earn monopoly profits and to overpay executives, all of whom had somehow managed to avoid having international recruiters pound on their doors during their tenure in the public sector.

4. By avoiding restructuring, the government created a tangle of regulatory and competition policy problems that have been the subject of some of the earlier lectures in this series, and to which I now turn, with special reference to recent American experience in the electric industry.

In my country, as in yours, we are on the verge of an era in which it should be possible for all electricity customers to shop for supplies, mercifully reducing the need for direct regulation, at least in the generation sector. Entry into the generation business is now technically possible, especially in this era in which low-priced natural gas combines with new technologies to make a nonsense of old arguments that there are overwhelming economies of scale in power generation. And, perhaps after some irritating delays of the sort you seem to be facing here, billing and other arrangements will be sorted out.

So natural barriers to entry and customer-billing problems are not barriers to competition in electric supply. In my country, the principal barriers to competition are four:

1. *Stranded assets.* Ours is an industry characterised by vertically integrated suppliers operating pursuant to monopoly franchises in specified geographic areas known as service territories. All utilities have an obligation to serve all comers, pursuant to which they built expensive plant in anticipation of demand which, in many cases, did not materialise. So long as the utility operates under the protection of its monopoly franchise, it can charge prices high enough to permit it to recoup its investments, and a reasonable return thereon, assuming, of course, that the investments were prudently made – again, a subject for another paper. Allow

competitors to enter, offering prices based on low-cost, gas-burning generating equipment, and the incumbents will have what has come to be called 'stranded assets' – to the tune of billions of dollars. And they will also be burdened with still more unrecoverable costs in the form of high-priced power purchase contracts, often signed at the insistence of the regulators. To force them to swallow these costs, argue the incumbent utilities, would be unfair, since the now-excess capacity was built pursuant to a social contract between regulator and regulated: you invest enough to serve all possible customers, and we will allow you a reasonable return on your investment. I have elsewhere analysed the economic and equity issues surrounding the arguments about 'stranded investment';[10] what is relevant here is that the presence of this stranded investment is the source of the American utilities' bitter fight to delay the introduction of competition in retail markets. And with good reason. The mere consideration of a competitive model by California's regulators caused a 20–30 per cent sell-off in the shares of the state's utilities. Indeed, if the generating assets of electric utilities were marked to market – valued at what they would be worth if the power they produce were sold at competitive prices – many US utilities would have negative book value.

2. *Vertical integration*. The second barrier to competition is the vertically integrated structure of the electric utility industry. New entrants into power generation must move their electricity over transmission and distribution wires owned by the very utilities with whom they aim to compete. With reason, they worry that the

---

10 'Stranded Investment. Who Pays the Bill?', remarks delivered at the Southeastern Electric Exchange, 30 March 1994 (mimeo).

terms and conditions of access might be so stringent as to make it impossible for them to compete, even though they are more efficient at generating electricity. As Harvard Professor William Hogan, who has studied this problem more intensely and intelligently than any American observer, noted in a privately circulated but not confidential memorandum, '... Competition in generation can be sensitive to the transmission and pricing rules.' In recognition of that fact, the Federal Energy Regulatory Commission, which regulates the interstate transmission of power, has hit upon the rule of 'comparability'. Broadly stated, this means that any vertically integrated utility that comes before the Commission to have a merger approved, or for almost any reason, must agree to move the power of any competitor on terms comparable with those on which it transmits the power produced by its own generating stations.

This is a solution that might commend itself to your Monopolies and Mergers Commission when it examines the proposed reintegrating mergers now before it. It certainly has considerable support in many segments of the American industry and in the regulatory community. But I would urge the MMC to consider, too, the possibility that comparability is unattainable. The dimensions of wires service are complex; the owners of the wires have a strong incentive to manipulate the terms of access when they also own generation facilities; and, as John Vickers reminded us last week, 'A vertically integrated firm that dominates one level of production has an obvious profit incentive to distort downstream competition by raising rivals' costs and discriminating in favour of its own downstream unit.'[11] Professor Vickers went on to note,

11   John Vickers, 'Competition and Regulation. The UK Experience', Institute of Economic Affairs Lectures on Regulation, London, 30 November 1995, p. 8 (mimeo).

'if conduct regulations were perfect and costless, the anti-competitive behaviour problem could be solved without resort to structural remedies. But it isn't so.' And this is not to criticise the regulators. Information asymmetry disadvantages them; as does an enormous difference between the resources available to the regulated and those at the disposal of the regulator; as does the inherent difficulty of defining the service that is being regulated, costed and priced. In the end, if emerging competition at the retail level is not to be strangled at birth, structural separation of the generating and wires businesses will probably prove necessary where there is substantial market power at either vertical level. And just such separation has been proposed by several American utilities as part of a 'grand bargain', the quid pro quo being permission to recover their stranded investment.

So, too, in the telephone industry. So long as BT controls the telecoms network, two problems, both insoluble, will bedevil the regulators. The first is the terms on which competitors should be granted access. The second is determining the dividing line between fair and unfair competition, between vigorous competition and predation, between practices that protect a market position and those that erect unreasonable barriers to entry. Don Cruickshank's willingness to seize the poisoned chalice of monitoring BT's competitive behaviour is admirable, but it represents, I fear, the triumph of hope over experience – experience with efforts to regulate vertically integrated companies.

3. *The greens.* The third barrier to emerging competition in America's electric supply industry is the political clout of the environmental movement. So long as each utility had a monopoly of its service territory, it could acquiesce in the demands of

environmentalists for a host of economically inefficient conservation arrangements, and for wider use of environmentally
benign but high-cost power supply technologies. After all, the costs
could be passed on to captive customers. But times have changed.
Competition from new, low-cost producers makes continuation of
the anti-consumer, utility/environmentalist alliance impossible.
So the environmentalists have enlisted in the anti-competition
cause, or at minimum are demanding that a 'green surcharge' be
added to prices imposed on new power producers for the use of
transmission and distribution wires. I believe you will find similar
pressures developing in Britain if competition forces incumbent
suppliers to cut back on environmental expenditures.

4. *State regulators*. The fourth barrier to competition is the state
regulator. These regulators, many elected to office, worry that
competition will benefit only large, industrial customers, who can
threaten to move their plant or expand in some other state; lower
rates to these customers, they worry, will force utilities to recoup
lost revenues from the small householder who does not have much
bargaining power. So, in many states regulators have specifically
rejected the idea of subjecting the utilities they regulate to competition from outside suppliers.

Despite these obstacles, competition is breaking out all over.
Large customers have begun shopping for power supplies, and are
being offered substantial discounts. Some regulators are considering how to develop more competition in wholesale markets, with
California serving as the battleground for those who would force
all generators to sell into, and all customers to buy from, a pool,
and those who would allow bilateral deals between customers,
producers, brokers and aggregators.

This dispute, of course, is simply a specific variant of the old, general argument about the virtues of co-ordination v. competition, with co-ordination advocates having the advantage of seeming to be able to predict the consequences of their proposals, while market advocates cannot. But, in my view, that is precisely why market advocates should prevail: their inability to predict the results of competition stems from the fact that those results will be determined by consumers expressing their price and quality preferences in unpredictable ways. It is they who will decide how much power is needed, where, at what prices, and in what combination of firm and interruptible supplies. Central planners need not apply.

Questions of how to apply competition policy have not yet arisen, but will soon: the Antitrust Division of the Department of Justice has only now begun to take a serious interest in the electric utility industry. That interest has been reflected, first, in a greater inclination to examine the competitive impact of the mergers that are occurring in the utility industry. It is reflected, second, in queries about the operation of some of the regional power pools, and in particular the terms on which the co-operating competitors who are members of the pool are willing to make transmission and other services available to non-members. Remember: in America the Federal Energy Regulatory Commission and state regulatory bodies have, in a sense, primary jurisdiction in these matters. But the heightened interest of the competition authorities should increase the weight given to competitive impacts by the regulators.

Let me now summarise the five lessons to be gleaned from American regulatory experience:[12]

12 In this connection, see my 'Two Styles of Regulatory Reform', *The American Enterprise*, March/April 1990, pp. 70–7.

1. *Structure matters*. Business historian Thomas McCraw put it well in his wonderful study of regulation and regulators: 'More than any other single factor ... underlying structure of the particular industry being regulated has defined the context in which regulatory agencies have operated.'[13] Both British and American experience suggest that a vertically integrated monopoly is the most difficult of all beasts to regulate: integrated companies can use the natural monopoly of their transmission grids – gas pipelines, electric transmission lines, the telephone network – to deter entry into other strata of the business.

2. *Competition matters*. Even limited competition provides regulators with some benchmarks against which to measure the performance of a dominant firm; gives consumers some alternatives; spurs the dominant firm to reduce costs, improve service, and innovate.

3. *People matter*. In the regulatory game, people matter. While regulators are limited by the economic forces at work at any time, their biases, intellects and perseverance can affect the regulatory process in important ways. In America, Alfred Kahn's penchant for economically sensible pricing was a powerful force for rate restructuring in the electric business, and his preference for competition hastened the demise of airline regulation. In Britain, Sir Bryan Carsberg rose above his training as an accountant to adopt an economist's attitude towards such concepts as cost. So far, Britain has managed to find a set of quite able, fair-minded

---

13 Thomas K. McCraw, *Prophets of Regulation*, the Belknap Press of Harvard University, Cambridge, MA, 1984.

regulators. Americans have little to offer by way of suggestions for improvement.

4. *Procedure matters*. Open processes add credibility to the result, and give regulators access to varying points of view. Expedition at the expense of a full presentation of all viewpoints is very dearly bought.

5. *Profits matter*. A regulatory formula that ignores the profit levels it produces cannot survive politically. Nor should it, for a formula that produces profits that are inadequate to attract capital will result in a derogation of service, and one that produces monopoly profits will unduly enrich shareholders and managers at the expense of customers. This may be why Britain's regulators have been driven to an explicit examination of the cost of capital in determining a proper figure for X. But this obscure and merely tangential use of profits in the regulatory formula still leaves regulators open to the charge of condoning excess profits – a not unreasonable reaction from a public untutored in the arcane niceties of regulatory computations.

Finally, I would like to touch briefly on competition policy, since I believe there are important lessons to be learned from US experience. These are:

1. Competition policy functions best when it is not overlaid with other objectives. If a practice is anti-competitive it should not be condoned; for example, because it creates jobs, since such jobs will exist at consumer expense and will in the long run make the economy less competitive in world markets. Nor should mergers that

create dominant firms be justified on the basis of a need to create 'national champions' to compete in world markets. If such 'champions' can't compete at home, they won't in the long run be able to compete abroad.

2. Competition is desirable in and of itself, and not only because it produces an efficient allocation of resources, or because multiple players, particularly in industries subject to rapid technological change, are likely to produce a greater variety of products and services, at lower cost, than is a single, all-dominant firm. It is desirable, too, because (a) it eliminates the need for government to set prices and otherwise involve itself in business matters; (b) it diffuses private economic power and creates an atmosphere that encourages entrepreneurs to take the risk of challenging incumbents, who they know will be restricted only to responses stemming from their efficiency, rather than their sheer power; and (c) it produces enough players to minimise the political power of the largest firm.

3. Certainty is not attainable, at least not if competition policy is to remain a flexible instrument. A few *per se* rules are possible, the outlawing of conspiracies to fix prices being the most notable. But attempts to limit market shares penalise success, and attempts to ban certain competitive practices, without inquiring into their competitive impact, stifle competition. In the end there is no avoiding a careful analysis of competitive impact, on a case-by-case basis.

4. A modicum of predictability is attainable. This necessarily means that a body of precedent must be developed to provide

some guide to businessmen and their counsel, some means of separating acceptable from unacceptable behaviour. The deliverers of such decisions carry the burden of being clear and explicit, of carefully setting forth their reasons for rejecting this argument, for adopting that one, for defining a market one way and not another. A simple recitation of each party's contentions, followed by unexplained conclusory paragraphs, is not enough.

I hope these few remarks have not offended you. It is always difficult for an outsider to be in the position of telling an audience that 'we do it differently, and better, where I came from'. That has not been my intention. Indeed, it is we who have borrowed from you the notion of introducing more incentives into the regulatory system, and we who are trying to benefit from your experience with a power pool as we restructure our own electric utility industry. So my goal was merely to offer you a few bits from the American system by way of reciprocation. I hope that I have succeeded, at least in small part.

Vertically integrated utilities: the regulators' poison'd chalice

This paper was presented at a Seminar on Vertical Issues in Public Utilities, sponsored by the Regulatory Policy Research Centre, Hertford College, Oxford, on 6 January 1997. It argues that vertically integrated utilities are difficult if not impossible to regulate, and that structural changes may often be the only way of achieving efficient performance where one horizontal level of an industry possesses substantial monopoly power.

It was my hope, when we first agreed that a paper on recent experience in the US electric industry might enrich a seminar on vertical integration in the utility industries, to present some empirical tests of the effect of vertical integration on various indicators of the vigour of competition. After all, in my country we now have fully integrated electric companies; we have companies that are spinning off some or all of their generation; and we have non-integrated generators. It would be wonderful to compare the performance, prices and profitability of these variously structured entities. Alas, we cannot – those familiar with my limited econometric skills will want me to substitute 'I cannot' for 'we cannot' – for three reasons.

First, not enough time has elapsed to give us a database that has any meaning. Indeed, some companies are still in the process of demerging, spinning off some or all of their generating plants, and concentrating on the 'wires business'. Others are remaining vertically integrated, and some of these are merging with neighbours, allegedly in search of economies of scale and scope but, in my view, more in the hope of becoming so big as to be immune to a hostile takeover. Still others are trying to become total energy companies by acquiring natural gas companies. Some electric utilities are diversifying into such lines of business as the provision of securities services, rounding up customers by pointing out that a burglary occurs every five seconds in America. The stated theory behind these purchases is that the customers of security services firms are potential customers of Western's energy and energy-related products and, in the case of the ADT acquisition, that the merger's successful conclusion will provide a well-known brand name that will facilitate the marketing of energy services.

Many utilities are making overseas acquisitions. Stated motives vary, and include a hunt for growth no longer seen as available in America's electricity market, the desire to gain experience operating in a competitive environment, or in foreign markets, and the hope of finding regulatory environments more benign than those in the United States. (The likelihood that these hopes will be realised would make an interesting subject for another paper.)[*]

All of these developments, most of them very recent, mean we do not have meaningful and readily classifiable performance data. Perhaps some day we will have a wonderful database with which to analyse the efficiency gains attendant upon these various strategies. But that day is yet to come.

A second reason why it would be difficult to assess the relative performance of variously structured companies is the fact that all price and cost data reflect the prevalence of excess capacity, what Harvard Professor William Hogan calls 'the hangover of old mis-

---

[*] Several American companies have disposed of their UK acquisitions. The tighter regulatory regime that replaced Lady Thatcher's 'light-handed regulation' made the UK market less attractive just as deregulation opened up new opportunities in America.

takes'. Lower prices, by this reckoning, cannot be taken as evidence of the benefits of competition or of some structural change in the industry; they may as well be attributable to the presence of excess capacity constructed years before reformers fired a whiff of competition across the industry's bow.

A third reason why an empirical analysis of the effects of vertical integration in the utility industries is not possible – and may never be – is that costs, prices and profits are determined by men, not markets – that is, by federal and state regulators. Low rates – that is, our American term for what in Britain are called prices – may be due to stricter-than-average regulation rather than better-than-average efficiency. High costs may be due to relaxed cost-plus regulation, or to regulators with a penchant for loading environmental costs on the companies they supervise. High profits may be due to managerial efficiency in bringing costs down, or to incompetent regulators who allow companies to over-earn relative to their costs of capital.

Even if it were possible to engage in some empirical comparison of, say, the performance of power stations owned by vertically integrated utilities and pure generators, I am not sure the exercise would tell us much about a future in which competition is scheduled to replace regulation in the generation sector. The more interesting question is what kind of performance we can expect in the future, under various assumptions about the vertically integrated nature of the electric utility industry.

So I fear you will have to bear with me while I share impressions rather than data with you, and rely on anecdotes rather than systematic data sets.

As many of you know, America's electric utilities own many large generating stations, among them many nuclear stations. It is worthwhile for students of the regulatory process to consider just how these plants came into being. Economists were forecasting that oil prices would soon reach $100 per barrel, and policy-makers were concerned about the Arabs' use of their so-called 'oil weapon' to cut off supplies of oil. So, oil was a disfavoured fuel. Natural gas, it was thought by Washington's energy planners, was likely to be a scarce resource, and as such should be reserved for its highest and best use, seen to be house-heating and cooking. So the federal government prohibited its use as a boiler fuel to generate electricity. Coal was considered a dirty, polluting fuel, especially in the Northeast, and its use interdicted or frowned on by the authorities. That left nuclear power, energy that was going to be 'too cheap to meter'.

The electric utility industry, of course, did not exactly resist the idea that nuclear was the wave of the future. After years of being considered stodgy, utility executives had an opportunity to be on the cutting edge of a new technology. And the regulatory system seemed to promise them a guaranteed return on any investment they made in this capital-intensive technology. Never mind that regulation only provided them with an *opportunity* to earn a fair rate of return on their investment; or that regulators might later decide that the investments being made were for some reason 'imprudent'. Nuclear was the fashion: it held out the promise of limitless supplies of electrical energy at prices immune from inflation, since those prices would be set largely with reference to the historic cost of the capital interred in the nuclear stations.*

---

* A similar infatuation with nuclear power is reflected in President George W. Bush's new (2001) energy policy, which proposes to subsidise nuclear plants because they are alleged to reduce reliance on foreign oil (not true), and to be free of greenhouse gases (true).

So we had a combination of bad forecasts; regulatory discouragement or outright prohibition of the use of oil, gas and coal; and a regulatory system that seemed set to reward the most capital-intensive technologies with a return on all investment, while penalising expense-intensive technologies by allowing only a flow-through of expenses into prices, with no profit add-on. Add to that a belief in economies of scale and the excitement of a new, quintessentially 'modern' source of electricity, and you get nuclear power.

In the event, many of these plants proved to be more expensive to build and to operate than originally thought. In part this was an inevitable consequence of the learning process associated with new technologies; in part it was due to the insistence by smaller utilities, with no opportunity to move up a learning curve, that they build and own one of these modern structures; in part it was due to the electric companies' reliance on contractors with little incentive to operate efficiently; in part it was due to the unhappy coincidence of unduly protracted licensing proceedings and a period of rapid inflation that drove nominal costs through the roof. One, budgeted at something like $245 million, cost $5.5 billion – and then never went into service, the victim of appalling business decisions, and of regulatory and political machinations that would make a wonderful novel, one in which the last chapter is being written as we sit here, as politicians, desperate to redeem a pledge of cheaper electricity for an important constituency, concoct a merger of Brooklyn Union Gas Company and the Long Island Lighting Company, with a quasi-state takeover to follow to permit the substitution of tax-free bonds for the existing debt, which bears a higher interest rate.[*]

---

[*] This transaction was eventually completed.

The prevalence of cost overruns such as this led to an acrimonious round of regulatory battles known as 'prudence reviews', from which few emerged with honour. Regulators who had enthusiastically supported nuclear power and issued certificates to electric companies to permit them to build these plants suddenly reversed field and disallowed some of the construction costs on the grounds that they were imprudently incurred. Utility executives who persisted in building these plants long after it became clear that they were an expensive alternative to fossil fuels or, so the greens promised, to conservation measures, argued that consumers should bear the full cost of these power plants. Environmentalists who had opposed the use of fossil fuels, the only realistic alternative to nuclear power, leaped in to criticise the companies that had tried to meet their obligations to serve by building 'clean' nuclear stations, suddenly deciding that they didn't like nuclear power either, and discovering sun and wind. And politicians who had meddled in markets – discouraging the use of fuel oil so as to reduce dependence on the Middle East; frowning on coal as a 'dirty' fuel; and controlling natural gas prices in a way that created a shortage, which shortage begat further intervention in the form of a prohibition on the use of natural gas as a boiler fuel – professed shock at the complicity of regulators and utility executives in the construction of nuclear power stations.

So much for background. The battles over what portion, if any, of the industry's investment in nuclear plants it should be allowed to recover in rates were mere skirmishes until recently. Generally, the state regulators disallowed some portion of the investment, or permitted the companies to amortise some of it without earning a return, but did not (with a few exceptions) adopt attitudes so punitive as to threaten the companies with bankruptcy. After all, each company retained a monopoly in its service territory, and did not have to fear that its rates would be so high as to threaten it with a significant migration of customers. Those few customers who might leave the area in pursuit of lower rates elsewhere, or might turn to self-generation, could be and were given special discounts. And if rates got high enough to attract the attention of politicians, special rates for the poor could be put in place. So there was no market constraint on the ability of companies to recover a good part of their investment in even very costly nuclear plants.

Then, everything changed. Technological advances produced small generating stations that could compete successfully with the giant central stations. Natural gas prices fell, making gas-fired generation attractive. To give you some idea of the problem faced by owners of capital-intensive plants, consider these very rough numbers. The full cost, including capital costs, of a nuclear plant is something like 7–11 cents per kilowatt hour. The full cost of a new gas-fired generator is 2.5–3 cents per kilowatt hour.

Obviously, if newcomers were permitted to compete, they could build plants that would produce electricity cheaply enough to win business from incumbents, unless those incumbents were willing to charge less than average total cost for their power, i.e. to write off a substantial part of their investment. In some cases even this would not be good enough: I am told that running costs of nuclear stations vary from less than 2 cents to more than 5 or 6 cents per kilowatt hour – and this does not include the on-going capital investments for which these plants seem to have an insatiable appetite. The lower-cost units can recover operating costs, plus a bit of a margin, competing with new gas-fired units; the higher-cost plants would have to sell at below marginal cost to continue operating if competition were given free rein or, if reason prevails over some regulatory fix-up, be shut down. Indeed, seven nuclear plants have been shut down in the past eight years, and several utilities are now agonising over decisions about whether to retire nuclear plants, perhaps even before their operating licences expire.[*] Anti-nuclear activists estimate that 25 of the nation's 110 nuclear reactors will be forced by competition to shut down; industry analysts put that number at closer to a half-dozen.

The industry's first reaction to this difficult situation was to deny newcomers access to transmission and distribution facilities, to use its vertically integrated structure to preserve its monopoly of generation. This position proved untenable, for several reasons, two of which are worth mentioning. The first is that the intellectual/political climate in America is mightily influenced by the success of airline deregulation and, to a lesser extent, natural gas deregulation. The notion that a regulatory system should deny customers the benefits of choice – customers who had flown to Hawaii for vacations at fares that only competition could produce – was untenable. And legislators and consumer advocates see no reason why the electric industry should be treated any differently from the natural gas industry, in which 25 per cent of residential customers will be able to select their own supplier by the year 2000.

Second, and more specifically, industrial customers and independent power producers led a political and regulatory assault on

---

[*] The increase in natural gas prices in 2000 and 2001 and the sale of some nuclear plants to new owners who did not reimburse the original owners for capital costs combined with improved operating performance of most nuclear plants to make these plants sufficiently competitive (capable of recovering operating costs plus some margin at market prices) to induce their owners to seek extensions of their operating licences.

the utilities' use of their control of the wires to restrain competition. These customers want to shop the country for electricity. They want to buy it from new suppliers, and they want to have it delivered to their factories. But the vertically integrated companies that own the delivery system – the transmission grid – are the same companies whose electricity is being displaced by the new power providers. Fortunately, the newly liberated shoppers have sufficient political clout to have persuaded Congress in 1992 to pass the Energy Policy Act, beginning the process of opening up transmission lines.

Keep in mind that in America we have both federal regulation of the interstate movement of electricity, and state regulation of intrastate sales. The division of authority is, needless to say, far from clear-cut, but it suffices for our purposes to know that at both levels regulators are groping for ways to allow competition to flower. Some 47 of the 50 state regulatory agencies have implemented or at least are considering plans to open their markets to competition,* while at the national level the Federal Energy Regulatory Commission has put pressure on owners of interstate transmission lines to grant access to all unaffiliated generators on the same terms that they grant access to their own generators.

So we have the federal regulators trying to open the transmission lines to non-integrated generators, and the regulators at the state level trying to do the same with distribution systems. But in both instances, regulators will be regulators, professing to believe in competition – and not insincerely – while at the same time wanting to retain control of the industry.

---

* The botched 'deregulatory' scheme in California, pursuant to which wholesale prices were deregulated but retail prices were not, is causing several states to review their plans to deregulate the utilities in their jurisdictions.

On the federal level, FERC is establishing cartel-like structures to manage the grid. More on that in a moment. On the state level, competition is being introduced on a controlled, phased-in basis, with first large and then progressively smaller customers eligible for freedom to choose. This desire to experiment to see if Adam Smith and successive generations of economists knew whereof they spoke, or wrote, is deemed appropriate prudence by regulators who view those calling for unbridled or unfettered competition (what, one wonders, is 'bridled' or 'fettered' competition?) as slightly mad. Competition, they worry, may result in inadequate capacity, or lower standards of reliability, or a lower standard of customer service – problems less blinkered folk associate with monopoly, not with competition, and which the regulated industry avoided, but only at enormous cost.

They worry, too, about the environmental consequences of more competition. For example, wide-open competition would result in lower-cost, coal-based power from the Midwest replacing more expensive nuclear power in America's Northeast. This, environmentalists contend, will add to pollution of all sorts, and increase the danger of global warming. Naturally, Midwestern producers don't agree: the CEO of American Electric Power argues that the Northeast's air quality problems stem from mobile sources (automobiles and trucks), and that his Northeastern colleagues' new concern with the environment is merely an attempt to prevent competitive power from entering their high-cost region.

And America's regulators are introducing such competition as they deem safe for the public to have only after paying a huge bribe. Let me explain. The lower costs available to new entrants left the incumbents with what has come to be called stranded investment. This is the investment in generating stations that cannot be recovered in prices if utilities are forced to match the prices on offer by new entrants. In most industries, such a situation would result in write-offs and even bankruptcies. But the utilities argued that they had made these investments in order to meet their legal obligation to serve all comers, and that they are therefore entitled to recover that investment. And, they add, some of their stranded costs result from high-priced purchase contracts imposed upon them by regulators eager to promote some favourite generating technique, such as geothermal steam, or solar energy; still more of these costs result from deferral of cost recoupment imposed by regulators and recorded on the books as 'regulatory assets'.

I have elsewhere dealt with the arguments concerning appropriate policy towards these various stranded costs, and won't bore you with a rehearsal of my analysis of the industry's position. Suffice it to say, many of the propositions advanced by the utilities are debatable; others, such as New England Electric John Rowe's contention that complete deregulation of all strata of the industry would leave no stranded costs, should appeal to the Chicago School devotees among you; still others, particularly those relating to the high-priced (above avoidable cost) power-purchase contracts imposed upon them, and to the regulators' promises to allow them to recover certain deferred costs, are not without their appeal.

Billions hinge on the outcome of this dispute over the treatment of stranded costs. But just how many billions it is difficult to determine. Many companies which claim that instant competition would be ruinous for them may quite possibly be correct. Take Texas as an example: regulators in that state estimate that the introduction of full competition by 1998 would create stranded investment totalling $14 billion.

But beware of these and other estimates of the calamity facing the industry. To predict just how much investment will be 'stranded' when competition rears its lovely head, we have to be able to predict the competitive price that will force the stranding. That means we have to predict the price of natural gas, the fuel predominantly relied upon by new entrants into the business, and of coal, the fuel primarily relied upon by those utilities eager to burst the bounds of their service territories and invade those of their now-higher-cost neighbours.

In the end, the level of stranded costs may not matter, since most regulators have decided to allow the utilities to recover all or a major portion of their now-uneconomic investments. Some do so for reasons of equity: the utilities, they reason, made these investments pursuant to a 'regulatory contract' that promised them a fair return as compensation for meeting the burden created by their 'obligation to serve'.

Other regulators allow stranded-cost recovery in order to get the utilities to stop their war against the introduction of competition, a war that the companies could protract by fighting the issue all the way up to the Supreme Court. Still other regulators are allowing recovery of stranded costs as part of a package that requires the utilities to continue environmental programmes that the market would force them to abandon if they were exposed to full-blown competition, and permits them to impose a wires charge on new entrants to provide funds to finance these uneconomic environmental adventures.

So deals are being cut, many of them in the British manner – largely out of public view, others so broadly consultative as to invite paralysis. These deals differ in detail, but are similar in broad outline. Some customers will be allowed to choose their suppliers. But utilities will be allowed to levy a competitive transition charge for the use of their wires, that charge to be paid by all customers, regardless of the source of their electricity, and used by the utilities to recover their uneconomic, stranded investment. So a customer who chooses a new supplier will have to pay a form of 'exit fee' – an extra charge, over and above cost (including a return on investment) for using his former supplier's wires – to compensate the utility for the cost of capacity being idled – even though that customer had no explicit contract to remain on the system; only customers who pack up their homes or factories and move to an area served by a different utility can escape this exaction. (Whether such a wires charge may be justified as having the effect of bringing transmission rates closer to the economically efficient level is a subject for another paper.)

That is the solution devised to solve the stranded investment problem – or at least that part of it that is relevant to our discussion today. And it is also in some instances part of the solution to the problem created by vertical integration. For in return for the establishment of a mechanism to permit stranded cost recovery, some utilities have agreed to spin off their generating plants, and confine themselves to the transmission and distribution businesses. Where such divestiture is complete, the price – stranded cost recovery – is said to be justified as being the bribe needed to get the utilities to agree to a more competitively structured industry.

Basically, the utility can sell its plants at market prices, which in many cases are well below book value, but will not have to write off the difference between book and market values because the competitive transition charge it will collect for the use of its wires will provide funds to make up the difference.

To cite two examples: the New England Electric System will spin off all of its generating stations. These include small pieces of five nuclear plants (two shut down for safety reasons) and fossil-fuelled and hydroelectric plants valued by the company at over $1 billion. Customers will be free to choose among competing suppliers, but will have to pay an access charge – a premium above cost – for the use of the wires needed to deliver their purchases. On the other coast, Southern California Edison will sell only some of its generating stations, and retain others. It expects to obtain more than book value for the ten fossil-fuelled plants being sold, and to use that excess to pay down the stranded investment created by the nuclear plants it will retain, thereby lowering the competitive transition charge that will be imposed on all users. Note that in the case of California, the bribe being paid did not purchase complete vertical divestiture.

Most utilities, however, are so far clinging to their vertically in-tegrated structures. Which, needless to say, creates a problem for independent generators who must have access to the utilities' wires if they are to compete with them. And must have access on terms that are more than merely non-discriminatory, a thought I will expand on in a moment.

But first let me acknowledge that the wisdom handed down from the economic mount – Chicago – is correct: vertical integra-tion itself does not necessarily pose a threat to competition. Un-less, in the presence of monopoly at one stage of the industry, regulation is not perfect, and leaves unexploited monopoly power in the hands of some companies. That this is the situation in the electric utility industry in America – and, I would venture to guess, in any country in which vertical integration by owners of the transmission and/or distribution systems into generation is permitted – only the most dedicated industry advocate can deny. Look at it this way: compare the regulatory problems that would exist in an industry in which generation was completely divorced from the wires monopolies with the problems we confront in the presence of vertical integration.

Utilities profess to solve this problem by offering their competitors in the generation business non-discriminatory access to their wires. But regulators quite properly worry about just how such a policy can be implemented. So, in an approach that reflects overweening faith in their skills at wringing every last ounce of unexploited monopoly power out of the system, they are asking the utilities to put their transmission grids – the utilities will retain ownership of the grids, thereby remaining vertically integrated – in the hands of independent system operators (ISOs), subject to regulatory scrutiny. These operators will match supply and demand by buying power from the lowest-priced supplier first, working their way up the supply curve as the quantity of power demanded increases. In most cases, all bids to buy and to sell must be placed with the ISO, presumably in the interests of co-ordinating use of the grid.

This leads to two obvious questions. First, stripped of control of their transmission asset, and regulated so as to earn only their cost of capital on that asset, why would utilities want to retain ownership, rather than spin off transmission, unless ownership continued to provide strategic advantages or regulation was considered incapable of preventing returns in excess of the cost of capital? The answer: they wouldn't.

Second question: how can a system operator, owned by a consortium of utilities, be truly 'independent' – indifferent as between its owners and independent sellers? To me, the answer is obvious: it can't. Especially since non-discrimination is not enough. As Professor Robert Willig of Princeton University has pointed out in the case of telecoms, a vertically integrated firm with a monopoly at, say, the distribution stage can offer a potential challenger in another part of its business treatment identical with that it provides itself, and, paradoxically, thereby bar entry. Often, the challenger needs some adjustment in the incumbent's technology – positive co-operation rather than an absence of discrimination. That will likely be the case of independent generators attempting to sell through an ISO to its ultimate customers. It is difficult to imagine a system operator, owned by incumbents, willing to be very helpful. Especially if that system operator happens to be saddled with several high-cost generating stations.

Our regulatory authorities have attempted to cope with this problem by setting up governance structures to guide the ISO. In establishing these structures, they are relying on proposals from the industry, and are calling for consensus – in fact, unanimity – among the players. The FERC wants all buyers and sellers in a market area to be represented on a systems operation committee, which committee will operate pursuant to a set of by-laws that FERC must approve, on the assumption that such a committee, so constrained, will produce – what? A compromise which may not have anything to do with maximising efficiency. And which will certainly not produce operating rules congenial to still more entry, or to the introduction of new technologies. I am reminded of John Vickers' 1993 Inaugural Lecture, in which he pointed out that one meaning of the phrase 'more competition' is 'a move away from co-operation or collusion towards *independent behaviour* between rivals'. How a governance system that requires competitors to reach unanimous decisions about issues such as pricing produces 'more competition' is not easy for an economist, especially one trained to be suspicious of what our antitrust authorities call 'facilitating devices', to understand. Here we have not competition as ordinary people understand the term, but regulators fashioning a new industrial order from the old by creating a central control room in which cartelists can spin dials to bring buyers and sellers together in a controlled environment by substituting neat technical expertise for reliance on messy markets.

It seems obvious to me that the only available efficiency-enhancing solutions contain two ingredients.

First, the stranded assets must be treated as markets treat all sunk costs – as irrelevant. Schemes to permit utilities to impose wires charges to recover investments that a combination of new technologies, cheap gas and free entry make uneconomic prevent prices from reaching marginal cost. Without such schemes, we will find that some existing plants will recover to investors all of the investment sunk in them; that some nuclear plants with low marginal operating costs will remain truly economic, and may even return to the investors some of the moneys invested in them – or a handsome profit if natural gas prices rise sufficiently to push up the operating costs of recent entrants; and that customers will be able to make efficient choices among competing sellers.

That, of course, is the economist's solution. But it may well be that a second-best alternative would be to allow some recovery of stranded costs in return for vertical divestiture – buy our way into a more competitive future, one which seems to me attainable only if the competitive generation business is divorced from the monopoly wires business. Understand: in my country stranded costs are a brooding omnipresence. Like the ghost of Hamlet, these costs demand to be recognised. Like the ghost of Hamlet, these costs demand that historic accounts be squared so that the poor souls now weighted down by them can pass from their present uncomfortable limbo to a more agreeable place. And, like the ghost of Hamlet, these costs will cloud a potentially glowing future until they are dealt with. So perhaps a decision to pay the bribe rather than torturing ourselves by hunting for the culprit – the person or body responsible for the incurrence of these costs – is the most rational choice.

The second ingredient in any sensible plan to introduce competition into the generating sector is vertical divestiture. Let me start with a concession: vertical integration probably reduces some transaction costs. Include a second concession: that in most instances entry barriers created by vertical integration are neither 100 per cent effective (in some cases there are alternative transmission paths), nor can be maintained forever. But neither of these arguments is available to those who would preserve the vertically integrated nature of the American utility industry.

Transaction costs between generators and the people who operate the wires are undoubtedly low, given the years of experience all parties have in co-ordinating supplies, economic dispatch and the like. And could be lower still if, as Columbia University law professor Richard Pierce, Jr, has pointed out, owners of various segments of the grid had unambiguous incentives to price their services efficiently, rather than to protect investments in generating assets.

More important, the likelihood that a new entrant will emerge in either the transmission or distribution businesses must also be deemed to be very low. That is not to say that there is no conceivable price at which it will pay someone to go through the arduous application process of building new transmission lines. Or that special circumstances, such as the possibility of building an underwater transmission line from Connecticut to Long Island,[*] might not create an opportunity for an independent transmission project. But if, as is likely in most cases, that independent construction would take place only where there are bottlenecks on existing systems, the entrant would have to have very active co-operation from the monopoly-transmitter to make his new facility of any use. Not likely.

And if the potential entrant into transmission decides to construct a complete, parallel system, he is unlikely to succeed, for reasons that should be obvious to all save those who believe a transmission tower is lovelier than a tree.

Distribution may be another matter. No new entrant is likely to tear up the streets to lay wires to compete with an incumbent, even one charging a very high monopoly price. And technologies that allow residential customers to generate power at or close to home are not sufficiently close to economic practicality to be a significant constraint on the exercise of monopoly power. But extensions into new developments may be open to competition – assuming the potential entrant can get the power to his boundary line, a feat that will require active co-operation from the incumbent.

All of this means that any independent generator knows that, standing between him and his potential customers, is an integrated competitor who will determine the terms on which the newcomer will have access to that customer. True, that vertically

---

[*] The state of Connecticut has vetoed this project, allegedly on environmental grounds, but more probably because it does not want electricity to move out of the state, causing in-state prices to rise.

integrated competitor will be regulated. And the regulator will attempt to see to it that the new entrant is granted access on non-discriminatory terms. But he will either fail, because the terms are too many and too complicated to be effectively reviewed by a regulator, or because non-discrimination is just not enough to assure access to customers.

The situation is exacerbated in the case of the US electric industry – as it is in most telephone industries around the world – by the fact that we are not here dealing with vertical integration by a new entrant, who may have to integrate to make an effective challenge to existing players. We are talking about vertical integration by incumbents who dominate not only the so-called 'natural monopoly' strata of their industry, but that level in which we are hoping competition will develop. As we have seen in the case of British Telecom, to cite only one example, incumbency matters: the long-time monopolists can count on customer inertia to offset the vigour of their new competitors. And on a policy of foot-dragging in developing procedures that facilitate entry by their challengers.

In short, I see no prospect of a truly competitive market for generation so long as monopoly owners of transmission and distribution wires are allowed to own generating plants. I base this conclusion, first, on the quite plausible assumption that the dimensions of transmission service are so complex that regulators will be unable to devise rules to guarantee truly non-discriminatory access; second, on the virtual certainty that the new ISOs, in the end operating under the surveillance of the utility owners of transmission facilities who possess great skills in gaming the regulatory process and who will have an information advantage over the regulators, will curry favour with owners of transmission systems by behaving like good cartelists; third, on the likelihood that even if such rules can be devised, they will not produce the affirmative co-operation that should be required of the owner of an essential facility; fourth, on the fear that the entry of integrated utilities into generating markets as 'independents' in the service territories of other utilities creates opportunities for mutual back-scratching that economists would call collusion; fifth, on the assumption that it is unrealistic to expect an integrated company to make its monopoly wires reasonably available to a generating competitor who might take business away from the integrated company, or force it to charge prices below average total cost or, worse still, to close down inefficient plants.

I look forward to learning whether this group feels that there are lessons here for other regulated industries. I would be inclined to derive one: anyone who hands to a regulator a vertically integrated, powerful incumbent with monopoly power at one stratum of the industry, along with the instruction to speed up the advent of competition, is handing him – or her – a poisoned chalice.

A review of privatisation and regulation experience in Britain

This lecture was delivered as part of the IEA/London Business School series of Beesley Lectures on Regulation on 7 November 2000 at the Royal Society of Arts, London. It will be published as one of the chapters in Utility Regulation and Competition Policy, *Colin Robinson (ed.), Edward Elgar (forthcoming). It was designed to demonstrate that regulation produces superior economic results to private monopoly power, and that competitive markets trump both.*

That the topics of privatisation and regulation should be linked is proof that monopoly power cannot be entrusted to private, profit-maximising corporations.* It must be placed under the control of the state, either through direct ownership, or by regulating its exercise. I shall in this lecture argue that regulation is a more efficient means of controlling monopoly power than is state ownership, that introducing competition is superior to both, but that merely chanting, in the manner of the Chicago School, that all monopoly power is transitory is to elevate hope over experience, or at a minimum to give a very generous definition to the number of years that can be included in the word 'transitory'.

But what I am about to say should not be taken as a failure to recognise that privatisation involves social costs, most notably those associated with the elimination of overmanning,[14] or a naive

---

*   Not all state enterprises need be monopolies; liberalisation, i.e. competition, is possible without privatisation; competitively structured industries are sometimes regulated. But this paper deals primarily with the privatisation of enterprises that are monopolies at the time they pass from state ownership.

14   For a discussion of these costs see Peter Self, *Rolling Back the Market: Economic Dogma & Political Choice*, Macmillan Press, London, 2000.

belief that regulation is a perfect process. As Alfred Kahn has pointed out in his magisterial work on the economics and institutions of regulation, 'Regulated monopoly is a very imperfect instrument for doing the world's work ... Regulation is ill-equipped to treat the more important aspects of performance – efficiency, service innovation, risk taking, and probing the elasticity of demand. Herein lies the great attraction of competition: it supplies the direct spur and the market test of performance.'[15]

The quality of regulation is limited not only by the intrinsic difficulty of substituting administrative processes for the marvellous self-regulatory tool we call the competitive market. It is limited as well by:

- the resource advantage that regulated companies generally have over the agencies charged with regulating them;
- the information asymmetry that gives the regulated an advantage over the regulator;
- the ever-present dangers of regulatory capture or, at the other extreme, the hostility that regulatory staffs often have for the companies they regulate;
- the abilities of the men and women chosen for the arduous task of substituting their judgements for that of the absent competitive market; and
- the abilities and interests of the legislators who create the framework within which regulators must operate.

---

15   Kahn, op. cit., vol. 2, 1971, pp. 325–6. (Reprinted in a single volume by The MIT Press, Cambridge, MA, 1988.)

This last point is especially important: the legal instruments handed to regulators by legislators often constitute a poisoned chalice, containing a brew that includes often-contradictory economic and equity potions, a dash of economic policy, a bit of social policy (subsidise this or that favoured group), and a large portion of political self-seeking (keep prices low and service quality high).

And the regulators themselves are of varying quality. I have known regulators who cannot distinguish a demand curve from a supply curve, and who think that marginal cost is the sum written in the margin of some accounting statement. I have dealt with others who are quite comfortable coping with the intricacies of econometric models (the best know just how many pinches of salt to take with their regression equations), and with various sophisticated techniques for measuring the cost of capital. I have dealt with regulators who engage with intellectual integrity in the difficult search for answers that maximise efficiency and fairly balance the interests of consumers and investors, and with others who search only for the answers that will require more staff and prolong their tenure in office. This experience inclines me to agree with one leading scholar that 'Individual persons ... have mattered a great deal in regulatory history.'[16] I know that the constitutionalists among you like to think that your government – and mine – are governments of laws, not men. But even a brief descent from an ivory tower should convince them that both matter, and in the case of regulation it may be men that matter more.

Regulation, in short, is not a perfect instrument for controlling

---

16   McCraw, op. cit., p. 303.

private monopoly power. But it seems to serve the public interest better than does state ownership. To reach that conclusion, of course, requires two judgements – one ideological, the other economic.

On the ideological side there is the usual room for differences of opinion. If one has a general bias in favour of limiting the role of the state, it will not take elaborate comparative efficiency studies to persuade you to come down on the side of private as opposed to public ownership. If one generally favours stronger rather than weaker trade unions, one will inevitably favour a greater role for public ownership, since the politicians who ultimately control publicly owned enterprises are more likely to bow to the wishes of trade unions than are the managers who control the affairs of private-sector enterprises, presumably (although not certainly or always) in the interests of the shareholder-owners of the enterprise. To the extent that one believes that businesses should pursue non-economic, social goals, one will favour public as opposed to private ownership. And to the extent that one is certain that regulation of privately owned monopolies is doomed to failure, perhaps because 'regulatory capture' is inevitable, one will prefer that monopoly enterprises remain in state hands, that being the lesser evil than unconstrained private power.

That considerations such as these, rather than a pure drive for greater economic efficiency, were a – some might well say 'the' – driving force behind Britain's privatisation wave few can doubt. One clear goal was to reduce the role of government in the economy and therefore in the lives of British subjects. That goal was achieved. Between 1979 and 1992 the portion of total employment accounted for by state-owned enterprises fell from 8 per cent to 3 per cent, the portion of output from 10 per cent to 3 per cent, and the portion of total gross domestic fixed capital formation from 16 per cent to 5 per cent.[17] All in all, state assets totalling some £45 billion were sold off.[18]

Another was to create a political force to offset the trade unions. Prime Minister Thatcher, as she then was, made no secret of her desire to alter the balance of political power by creating a 'share-owning democracy',[19] with more shareholders than there were trade union members.[20] This goal, too, was achieved. When the privatisation programme began, there were 3 million shareholders and 13 million trade union members in Britain. Today, there are almost 13 million direct shareholders, and fewer than 8 million trade union members. Needless to say, the achievement of the Thatcherite objective of creating a new shareholding class did not ensure permanent Tory tenure at 10 Downing Street. But it may be one reason for the 'New' in New Labour – the people, either in their roles as consumers and investors, or through their regulatory bodies, may well be closer to controlling the commanding heights of the economy than they were when the several 'barons' ran the nationalised coal and other industries.

---

17 Michael G. Pollitt, 'A Survey of the Liberalisation of Public Enterprises in the UK Since 1979', University of Cambridge, Department of Applied Economics working paper, January 1999, p. 1. The most notable remaining public enterprises are the Post Office and the London Underground.

18 David Parker and Stephen Martin, 'The Impact of UK Privatisation on Labour and Total Factor Productivity', Working Papers in Commerce, University of Birmingham, 24 November 1993, p. 2.

19 Seth Thomas, 'The Privatisation of the Electricity Supply Industry', in John Surrey (ed.), *The British Electricity Experiment. Privatisation: The Record, the Issues, the Lessons*, Earthscan Publications Ltd, London, 1996, p. 41.

20 'The encouragement of share ownership, especially by company employees, was another major goal of the program . . . ' John Vickers and George Yarrow, *Privatisation: An Economic Analysis*, MIT Press, Cambridge, MA, 1988, p. 159.

It was the pursuit of the goal of creating a shareholder class which led to the underpricing of the shares of to-be-privatised companies. The theory was quite simple: underprice the shares of such enterprises as British Telecom and British Gas so that the small shareholders (the so-called 'Sids') to whom shares were allocated at the time of privatisation – allocation being necessary because the underpricing resulted in oversubscriptions – would immediately see the value of their shares rise. This would persuade them to become active capitalists in the future, and to support the free-market, low-tax and other policies of the Conservative Party. The fact that huge values had been transferred from taxpayers to shareholders[21] was not deemed troublesome, and was anyhow remarked upon only by economist/quibblers whose voices were drowned out by the clanging of tills in the offices of investment bankers and the cheers of new shareholders. Not to mention the applause of the managers of the newly privatised enterprises, men (almost no women) who suddenly realised just how valuable they were, and proceeded to adjust their compensation accordingly, this being a time before shareholders became somewhat more aggressive in attempting – so far with only indifferent success – to relate compensation to performance.

To the ideologue – and I include myself in the group of those who think that taking away from government those things that can be done by the private sector is intrinsically a good thing – privatisation, then, was a success. It pushed back the frontiers of the

---

21 Discounts, the difference between the price at which the government sold the shares of 'the major natural monopoly privatisations' and the prices at which they were initially quoted, ranged from 20 per cent in the case of power generators to 86 per cent in the case of BT. Mike Wright and Steve Thompson, 'Divestiture of Public Sector Assets', in Jackson and Price, op. cit., p. 55.

state. It reduced the power of ministers over many industries. It created a new class of shareholders.

To the economist, too, privatisation was a success, although it must be noted that the evidence concerning the economic differences between the efficiency of various industries when in state ownership, compared with performance after privatisation, does not point unambiguously in one direction.

That evidence is in any event not easy to appraise. For one thing, it is somewhere between difficult and impossible to separate the effects of privatisation from the effects of such things as trends in the economy. For another, measuring productivity remains more art than science, as those now engaged in the debate over whether we have a 'new economy' or merely the same old one in the midst of a productivity-enhancing cyclical upturn are finding out.[22] Most important, 'It can be argued that the degree of product market competition and the effectiveness of regulatory policy typically have rather larger effects on performance than ownership *per se*.'[23] So, simple before-and-after analyses of labour or total factor productivity cannot be considered conclusive.

Which is why a survey of the literature throws up some evidence that challenges the proposition that privatisation resulted in important improvements in efficiency. David Parker, reviewing several studies that compare the performance of public- and private-sector companies, reports, 'It is difficult to see what general conclusion can

---

22 In this connection, see my 'Crash or Boom? On the Future of the New Economy', *Commentary*, October 2000, pp. 23–7, and several recent studies by Goldman Sachs.

23 Vickers and Yarrow, op. cit., p. 3.

be drawn from this record.'[24] Michael Pollitt, comparing the pre- and post-privatisation performance of several firms, concludes, 'Privatisation itself does not seem to be associated with an acceleration of productivity growth or profitability.'[25] The key word here is 'itself'. It seems that it is the introduction of competition where that is attainable, and efficient regulation where elements of natural monopoly remain, that account for the improvements in efficiency that followed the entry of several firms into the private sector.

But it must be remembered that the liberalisation of many of the markets occurred precisely because the government no longer had a stake in preserving the monopoly positions of the one-time nationalised firms once they were no longer state owned. So, although competition or regulation produced the efficiency gains, the privatisation of the enterprises was a necessary predicate to the introduction of competition where feasible, and regulation where necessary. In fact, it might be well to think of the history of these firms in three phases.

1. As state-owned enterprises: the firms looked to the government to protect them from competition and to subsidise them when they couldn't cover their costs.
2. As firms operating during the period immediately preceding privatisation: the government was seeking to maximise the value of the enterprises' shares, to the extent that was consistent with its desire for widespread share ownership. It therefore had a continued stake in preserving some of the

---

24 David Parker, 'Nationalisation, Privatisation, and Agency Status within Government: Testing for the Importance of Ownership,' in Jackson and Price, op. cit., p. 150.

25 Ibid., p. 23.

monopoly protections enjoyed by the firms – the grant of so many Heathrow slots to BA is one example, the preservation of British Gas's vertically integrated structure is another, the preservation of BAA's monopoly of airports serving London still another – and in promising that regulation would be merely 'light handed'.

3. As firms operating after privatisation: the government generally came to realise that if consumers ('voters' in the politicians' jargon) were to get some semblance of value for money, and something approximating a quality service, competition or effective regulation was required.

And it does seem to be the case that once competition and/or effective regulation was introduced, performance improved markedly. Real operating costs declined at a compound annual rate of 3.7 per cent in the water industry, 4.1 per cent in the sewerage industry, 6.5 per cent in the transmission of electricity, 6.8 per cent in electricity distribution, and 9.1 per cent in gas transportation.[26]

But I hasten to emphasise again that the literature is not unanimous. Indeed, the very report that I have cited includes data that show that the rate of increase in total factor productivity of several privatised companies declined after privatisation.[27] My own conclusions after a meander through the literature, and first-hand observation of some industries, are as follows:

---

26 'Review of Railtrack Efficiency', *European Economics*, 9 December 1999, p. 15.

27 Ibid, p.18. That may, of course, have been the consequence of a pre-privatisation spurt in efforts to spruce up these firms' performances in order to increase their market values. Parker and Martin found that 'in most cases a performance improvement occurred in the run-up to privatisation, suggesting rationalisation by management in anticipation of having to survive in the private sector'. Op. cit., p. 19.

1. Privatisation was the first step on a long road to improving the efficiency of the nationalised industries.
2. In many cases the road was made rockier by the government's failure to consider the form of privatisation that would most likely maximise competition and minimise the burdens placed on regulators.[28]
3. When competition or effective regulation was introduced, many dimensions of performance improved. These gains included better financial performance,[29] a reduction in overmanning, and an increased responsiveness to customer demands, either because competition induced it, regulators mandated it, or government ministers changed from industry protectors into industry critics.
4. An important aspect of privatisation has been the conversion of managers from agents acting for their government departments to agents acting for their shareholders; the substitution of options and bonuses for honours as a motivating force; and the substitution of capital markets for ministerial largesse as a source of capital. An electric supply industry beholden to the government for funds was certainly more likely to make a deal to sustain inefficient coal producers than one subject to the discipline of capital markets, although vestiges of the old pressure to protect mining jobs certainly remain, at a high cost to the environment and the efficiency of the supply industry. A

---

28 In this connection see, for example, Colin Robinson, 'Privatising the Energy Industries: The Lessons to be Learned', *Metroeconomica*, vol. XLIII, nos 1–2, February–June 1992; and Robinson's 'Profit, Discovery and the Role of Entry: The Case of Electricity', in Beesley, *Regulating Utilities*, op. cit. 'In electricity, as in other privatisations, a good idea has been imperfectly executed' (p. 109).

29 Pollitt, op. cit., p. 23.

telecoms CEO who has to please investors is likely to behave differently and to hone different skills from one whose goal is to please ministers, although the increase in efficiency, profitability and quality of service may be some time in coming.

Perhaps the best current example of the difference between private- and public-sector operation is provided by the media industries. The BBC, admittedly woefully inefficient, and steadily losing market share, is rewarded by government with an increased flow of funds confiscated from taxpayers, despite its clear dilution of its public-service broadcasting obligations, and a drive to expand in areas where no market failure can be found to justify such expansion. Efficiency is unnecessary; clear corporate goals are unnecessary; satisfying viewers is unnecessary. Indeed, even cocking a snook at the responsible minister proves no impediment to unlimited funding.

Contrast that with a private-sector broadcaster. A performance such as that of the BBC would result in reduced access to funds, another way of saying that funds would gravitate from the company that failed to satisfy viewer needs and wants to those that succeeded in doing so. Economists call this the more efficient allocation of capital.

As I have already pointed out, privatisation was a necessary but not sufficient condition for the attainment of these gains. True, as a matter of theory some of the advantages of privatisation – reliance on capital markets, creation of incentives for managerial and worker efficiency – might be obtained within the nationalised structure. But history suggests that these advantages were not often achievable in practice, although where competition was introduced nationalised companies did respond by becoming more efficient.[30] And the history of these companies since they entered the private sector encourages the belief that privatisation was indeed a key factor, if for no other reason than it set the stage for a more competitive or more effectively regulated industrial environment.

Which brings me to the next phase of this paper. I would like to take the few remaining minutes to appraise the way in which regulation and competition have developed in the industries that were once state owned. This appraisal starts with a bias, and proceeds to a set of impressions – no claim is made for the systematic or scientific nature of what follows.

The bias is this: competition does a better job than regulation in producing a variety of goods and services, at prices that are most closely related to costs that are themselves minimised by competitive pressures. At least some of you are familiar with the virtues of competition as set forth in the various economic textbooks to which those of you fortunate enough to have studied the dismal science were exposed in your formative years; I need not repeat them here in any detail. Competition in product markets forces firms to give consumers what they want at acceptable prices; it allocates capital and other resources to their best use; within any given distribution of income, it maximises welfare; and it creates a fairer and more stable society, one in which

---

30 For example, the Post Office seems to have become more efficient as competition has become more intense. 'We found that when the competitive environment became tougher, *tfp* [total factor productivity] increased significantly. Strikingly, this was as true of those firms which have remained in public ownership, notably the Post Office, as for those that have been privatised.' Matthew Bishop and Mike Green, 'Privatisation and Recession – The Miracle Tested', Discussion Paper 10, Centre for the Study of Regulated Industries, London, 1995, p. 33.

opportunities to exploit one's talents are not foreclosed by monopoly power.

That is why attempts to regulate industries in which effective competition is possible – because of the notion either that competition would threaten product quality, or safety, or that it would produce unacceptable discrimination among customer classes, or prevent the subsidisation of groups favoured by politicians – have generally produced disastrous results. As Alfred Kahn has put it in his discussion of 'the deregulation revolution' that has swept through America's airline, trucking and bus industries, its stock exchange, and to some lesser extent our cable industry:

> About most of these a consensus was already emerging in
> the early 1970s among disinterested students that regulation
> had suppressed innovation, sheltered inefficiency,
> encouraged a wage/price spiral, promoted severe
> misallocation of resources by throwing prices out of
> alignment with marginal costs, encouraged competition in
> wasteful, cost-inflating ways, and denied the public the
> variety of price and quality choices that a competitive
> market would have provided.[31]

The appropriate public policy for these industries is relatively easy to arrive at – deregulate and rely on markets, preserved in their competitive state by a vigorous antitrust policy when necessary. It is when we have to deal with industries in which some mixture of regulation and competition is required – industries in which producers are not yet pure price-takers, or industries in which one horizontal level has natural monopoly elements – that

---

31   Introduction and postscript to the 1988 reissue of Kahn, *The Economics of Regulation*, op. cit., p. xvi.

the problems arise. In such industries, complex judgements concerning when to intervene and when to leave things alone must be made. Regulators must decide:

- when a price run-up constitutes the manipulation and the exercise of market power, and when it merely reflects supply and demand conditions and the responses to them of competing sellers;
- when vertical integration will reduce transactions costs and generate savings that will be passed on to consumers, and when it will create distortions at other horizontal levels of the industry;
- when intervention in response to short-run problems such as price 'spikes' is appropriate, and when such action will create long-run disincentives to new entry; and
- when mandating access to bottleneck facilities will increase the rate of innovation and the pace of new entry, and when it will discourage investment in such facilities.

In these instances in which the regulator must balance his desire and the pressure upon him to intervene against that small, inner voice that attempts to remind him what he has learned about the superiority of market forces, the temptation to intervene can become irresistible. Not for most regulators Ronald Reagan's advice: 'Don't just do something, stand there.' As Kahn has put it, 'In making complex judgments like these, the anti-competitive bias of the regulatory mentality has ample opportunity to manifest itself.'[32] After all, if the regulator decides in favour of a

32   Ibid., vol. 2, p. 114.

monopoly structure as opposed to a competitive one, he in effect has created a chosen instrument to which he guarantees freedom from competition in return for obedience to his views on prices, the desired quality of service, and the social functions it should accept as part of the 'deal' with the regulator.

It is the importance of what Kahn calls the regulator's 'mentality' which lends weight to my view that the quality of regulation is often a function of the quality of the regulator, and of the legislative tools given to him by the politicians. If the regulator has a bias in favour of competitive solutions, and if the legislative structure within which he must work permits him to exercise that bias, regulation is likely to work better than if these two conditions are not met. So let me spend a moment examining, first, the tools available to Britain's regulators, and then the way in which the regulators have used these tools.

The tools

It must be remembered that when it launched the programme of privatising firms that were to retain substantial monopoly power, Britain had no significant experience with economic regulation or regulatory agencies on the scale that privatisation would necessarily engender. All talk was of 'light-handed regulation', of tiny regulatory bodies with small budgets and few staff, and of avoiding 'American-style adversarial litigation'. Such was the stuff that Tory dreams were made of.

In the event, the government was heading down a path that would involve the creation of an entire new branch of government, agencies with enormous power over the fate of key industries and over the prices that consumers would pay for important necessities such as water, electricity and natural gas. Given the importance of the regulators' missions, and what Sir Bryan Carsberg has called the 'conflicting vested interests' that are inevitably involved,[33] it was somewhere between foolishness and wild optimism for the government to imagine that regulation is a process that can be performed by a few folks applying uncontroversial techniques to determine prices that will be fair to consumers and at the same time yield returns adequate, but no more than adequate, to attract capital in sufficient quantities to maintain service at acceptable levels.

The resources and tools bequeathed by the government to the regulators proved woefully inadequate, especially since the government paid little attention to the need to restructure the privatised companies so as to maximise the possibility of competition.[34] The problem was compounded – and I say this with all respect to our chairman this evening[*] – when antipathy towards 'American-style cost-plus' regulation, as it was mistakenly called here, led to reliance on the RPI-X formula. I have elsewhere commented on the failings of that formula, and will repeat here only two points. No one knew how to measure and to forecast 'X', the anticipated cost savings due to greater efficiency. And no one

---

33 Bryan Carsberg, 'Injecting Competition into Telecommunications', in Veljanovski, *Privatisation*, p. 81.

34 'It would have been possible, for instance, to have split British Telecom into a number of separate enterprises or ... to have sold the UK's two major international airports separately rather than privatising the British Airports Authority intact.' Michael Fleming and Kenneth Button, 'Regulatory Reform in the UK', in Kenneth Button and Dennis Swan (eds), *The Age of Regulatory Reform*, Oxford University Press, Oxford, 1989, p. 92. And there was no need to sell off British Gas as a vertically integrated monopoly, sowing the seeds for future regulatory problems.

* Professor Stephen Littlechild, the 'father' of RPI-X.

anticipated the political consequences of a formula that placed no effective and visible constraints on the profits that a monopoly utility might be permitted to earn.

When the newly privatised companies proved capable of wringing cost savings far in excess of anything contained in the 'X-files', profits soared, in some industries at the expense of service quality. So regulators found themselves in the difficult businesses of trying to force prices down so as to contain profitability, and of developing efficiency standards, a chore carried out with a wonderfully optimistic view of the power of regression equations, and to its highest level of detail by the water[35] and electricity regulators of those distribution networks.

This is not to criticise the individual regulators. In part, the evolution of the regulatory regime to something closer to the American model was predictable, and not a function of any failure on the regulators' part to implement the unrealistic expectations that regulation could be kept to a minor chore. The regulators had been given flawed tools. They had to overcome a huge information asymmetry problem, most notably in the early days of the regulation of the vertically integrated gas monopoly that the government of the day had seen fit to unloose on an unsuspecting public and on under-resourced regulators; and they had to overcome the residual arrogance of the 'barons' who ran the state-owned com-

---

35 The water industry provides a good example of the problems, as a reading of Ofwat's *1999 Periodic Review* reveals. First, the underestimation of potential efficiency gains: 'Since the 1994 price review, the companies have significantly outperformed the Director's expectations about how efficient they could become' (p. 27). Then profits hit unexpectedly high levels: 'The rates of return on capital have been high ...' (p. 31). Then the inevitable overreaction, driving profitability down to the point where several companies are attempting to extract their remaining equity capital from the industry.

panies and, backed by the trade unions, were accustomed to having their way with mere ministers and parliamentarians, not to mention regulators. Which brings me to my final subject: the regulators.

The regulators

The amazing thing to this long-time observer of the regulatory process in your country and mine is that the entire system did not collapse. The agencies responsible for regulating these key industries did not have adequate resources; the companies they were asked to regulate were not in a co-operative mood and proved unwilling to share data or concede that regulators had a legitimate role to play; the formula on which regulation was to be based was flawed.

Yet here we are, in the 21st century, with regulated utilities that are somehow continuing to function, and regulatory agencies that have grown in expertise. This is in large measure because, as I mentioned earlier, the people who get these jobs matter, and Britain has been fortunate in its selection of regulators. They have been truculent when necessary, attempted to maximise the scope of competition,[36] and wrestled with difficult conceptual problems with some success. It would be out of character for me to heap undiluted praise on regulators, so I

---

36 Many of Britain's leading regulators have been devoted to competitive solutions. 'Whenever I become aware of a problem … I ask first whether the problem can be alleviated by bringing about more competition or better competition.' Carsberg, op. cit., p. 82. 'Competition, whether existing or merely potential, is a vital protection for consumers against … higher prices, lower quality of service and reluctance of service and reluctance to innovate.' S. C. Littlechild, 'Ten Steps To Denationalisation', in Veljanovski, *Privatisation*, p. 18.

must add that their performance has not been without its flaws: the water industry may be suffering from overly constrained revenues; the electric industry is at the mercy of a regulator who believes he can separate good behaviour from bad;* the telecoms industry has not been opened up to competition as rapidly and completely as some would like. But all in all, given the difficulty of the chore of creating what is indeed an entirely new branch of government, it is fair to say that Britain's regulators should be given good marks, as I believe you say in this country.

Oddly, this seems to be truer of those regulators charged with overseeing the monopoly utilities – electric, gas and water distribution – than of those responsible for industries in which competition is more feasible. In the 'wire industries' – cable and telephony – regulators have been reluctant to mandate the open access that is necessary to break the competitive 'bottlenecks' that incumbents have set up. I recognise that the advantages of open access have to be weighed against the possible disincentive such access creates to investment in new facilities.[37] And that there is not unlimited capacity in the buildings of incumbent telephone providers to accommodate new entrants. But a re-examination of the balance being drawn between the desirability of lowering entry barriers and treating incumbents fairly might just produce a greater tilt in favour of more rapid market opening.

---

* The 'good behaviour' clause has since been struck down by the Competition Commission. It may emerge in a new guise at some later date.

37 For a concise discussion of the question of access, especially in the context of vertical integration, see Lars Bergman *et al.*, *Europe's Network Industries: Conflicting Priorities*, Centre for Economic Policy Research, London, 1998, pp. 24–7.

In the highly competitive broadcasting industry, where competition is distorted by the amazing ability of the BBC to extract ever-larger sums from taxpayers in pursuit of an ever-expanding role, and by generous spectrum grants to chosen instruments to the disadvantage of potential entrants, and where cultural considerations inevitably affect regulatory decisions, regulators nevertheless have greater freedom than they have chosen to exercise in promoting competition. Instead, we see a web of regulations stupefying in their complexity, often based on economically illiterate definitions of relevant markets, and aimed at favouring this or that competitor. Perhaps the White Paper that is due out this week will take scissors to all of this red tape and nonsense, and remove impediments to the rapid development of the new technologies that hold such promise. [Alas, it did not.] And perhaps some guidelines will be established to limit the BBC to specified areas, and thereby prevent that organisation from continuing to use the hoary anti-competitive tactic of pre-announcing services to discourage potential entrants. [Alas, they were not.]

Let me conclude with a thought on where the regulatory regime might go from here. First, all regulators should concentrate on getting the incentives right: you cannot create an incentive for punctuality by fining operators for late arrivals of trains, and hope that they will not respond by elevating punctuality over safety. You cannot induce efficient overall performance by creating incentives to lower one set of costs, and hope that the regulated companies will not meet that goal by incurring higher costs in other areas of their operations.

Second, where competition exists or is possible, the regulatory burden should be reduced. Note: the long arm of the regulator remains necessary where the invisible hand does not operate.[38] But in other places, every effort should be made to substitute competition for regulation, including in the so-called 'network industries', in which natural monopoly elements are of 'diminished significance' and in which 'encouraging competition generally leads to greater dynamism and welfare gains'.[39] After all, since Britain began creating regulatory bodies, two things have changed: many of the regulated companies now face at least some competition, and Britain has a new and more potent competition policy. The need for sectoral regulation has certainly diminished, although by just how much can only be determined by sector-by-sector study of the effectiveness of competition. Such studies must be undertaken in full awareness of what public choice theory teaches us – that regulators have a strong disinclination to declare victory and return to the academic, business or government careers from whence they came.

Third, regulatory procedures must be improved. In many instances they lack sufficient transparency; regulators do not adequately explain the basis for their rulings; there is no adequate appeals process that provides regulated companies with an alternative to the often hostile staffs of the regulatory agencies.

Finally, in the overlapping telecoms/media area, multi-forum regulation must be rationalised. As Professor Ian Hargreaves has pointed out, 'A system that currently involves ... 14 separate regulatory bodies, overseen by two government departments, must

---

38 'I would love to go down in History as the last energy regulator but I believe the gas and electricity markets will continue to need some regulation ... ' Callum McCarthy, Director-General, OFGEM, quoted in Keith Boyfield, *The Politics of Regulation*, European Policy Forum, London, 2000, p. 36.

39 Bergman *et al.*, op. cit., p. 39.

be unified. A regime sown with the risk of double jeopardy needs to be simplified, both in the interests of consumers and in the interests of business . . . '[40]

But that is a topic for another evening.

---

40 *Financial Times*, 25 May 2000.

3 THOUGHTS ON ENERGY AND ENVIRONMENT POLICY

Making environmental regulations: reconciling differing world views

This talk was delivered on 3 December 1997 at one of the policy conferences held annually by the American Enterprise Institute. Its purpose was to argue that policy disputes over environmental issues are difficult to solve because the parties to these disputes have very different world views.

Discussions of environmental issues often generate more heat than light – and for good reason: these debates are about strongly held and widely different views of how the world works, and how it should work. They are perhaps the most deeply ideological of any debates since the welfare state was established over the objections of those who believed in a much more limited central government. My hope is that in this little talk I can demonstrate that debates about this or that rule, or this or that figure in some cost-benefit analysis, are so intense because the world views underlying what seem to be discussions of regulatory details are, in fact, a clash of what Tom Sowell calls 'underlying assumptions about the world – a certain vision of reality'.[1] These visions, adds Sowell,

---

1   Thomas Sowell, *The Vision of the Anointed*, Basic Books, New York, 1995, p. ix.

'compete with one another . . . for the allegiance of . . . a whole society'.[2]

I think it not unfair to say that arguments about environmental policy are, in reality, arguments between people with competing visions about three fundamental issues: the desirability of economic growth, as such growth is conventionally but, alas, incorrectly measured;[3] the fairness with which the world's income is distributed; and the extent to which government should intrude on individual decision-making. In an attempt to elucidate these issues I have borrowed from political cartoonists, and will at times resort to caricature, and then compound that sin with a bit of generalisation.

Before doing so, however, let me summarise my own views on the issues before us. Some of my best friends are environmentalists. They have made a significant contribution to an improvement in the quality of American life at a cost not in excess of the value of the benefits, as best we can reckon. Thanks to them, our air is purer and our rivers cleaner.

That said, despite the fact that any fair-minded person must concede these accomplishments to the environmental movement, the world visions of environmentalists and those more sceptical of the need for further steps to improve our environment or to avoid future degradation remain wildly different.

---

2   Ibid.
3   The failure to include in reported GDP and incomes such non-market outputs as environmental quality and leisure time muddies this argument; discussion of this issue would require a separate paper.

Economic growth

The gap between what for purposes of this section of my talk I will call 'environmentalists' – I will later distinguish between those for whom environmental values are absolute, and other more nuanced thinkers – and those who have a presumption in favour of economic growth is substantial. The latter associate economic growth with rising incomes,[4] improved living standards, an increased willingness and ability of the 'haves' to share with the 'have nots', the ennobling impact of jobs for all, the spread of democratic institutions,[5] and even with improved environmental quality.[6]

Not so environmentalists. Economic growth, as they see it, places a strain on finite natural resources, in which are included everything from fossil fuels to clean air;[7] results in the production

---

4   See, for example, Adam Smith, *An inquiry into the Nature and Causes of the Wealth of Nations*, vol. 1, R. H. Campbell and A. S. Skinner (general eds), Clarendon Press, Oxford, 1976. Smith argues that countries experiencing a 'continual increase' in national wealth pay the highest wages (p. 87). Also, 'Though the wealth of a country should be very great, yet if it has been long stationary, we must not expect to find the wages of labour very high in it' (p. 89).

5   Robert J. Barro, *Determinants of Economic Growth: A Cross-Country Empirical Study*, MIT Press, Cambridge, MA, 1997, p. 61. '... non-democratic places that experience substantial economic development tend to become more democratic.'

6   '... the real secret to environmental improvement is economic growth.' Lee R. Raymond, Chairman and Chief Executive Officer of Exxon Corporation, speech at the World Petroleum Congress in Beijing, 13 October 1997. See also Thomas G. Schelling, 'The Cost of Combating Global Warming: Facing the Tradeoffs', *Foreign Affairs*, vol. 76, no. 6, November/December 1997, pp. 8–14. Schelling argues (p. 8) that the developing countries' 'best defense against climate change and vulnerability to weather in general is their own development ...'

7   The most famous modern-day statement of the position that 'present growth trends' are propelling us to disaster is, of course, the so-called Club of Rome study. Donald H. Meadows, Dennis L. Meadows, Jørgen Randers and William W. Behrens III, *The Limits to Growth*, Universe Books, New York, 1974, hereinafter

and accumulation of goods that people have been led to believe they need by insistent advertising,[8] rather than goods that satisfy 'the basic material needs of each person on earth';[9] and forces us to rely increasingly on fossil fuels that foul the environment[10] and makes us dangerously dependent on imports from unstable parts of the world.[11]

---

cited as Meadows *et al.* The fear that we will run out of resources did not originate with the Club of Rome, of course. Some 100 years earlier William Stanley Jevons, styled by Joseph Schumpeter (*A History of Economic Analysis*, Oxford University Press, Oxford, 1954, p. 826) as 'without any doubt one of the most genuinely original economists who ever lived', worried about 'our present rapid multiplication when brought into comparison with a fixed amount of material resources', and expressed the fear that Britain's industrial growth would come to a halt because its coal reserves were running out. Worse still, '... it is useless to think of substituting any other kind of fuel for coal.' W. Stanley Jevons, *The Coal Question*, Augustus Kelley, New York, 1965, in the series Reprints of Economic Classics, in this case of the third (1906) edition, pp. 183 and 454. Similar predictions of the impending exhaustion of the world's oil resources crop up periodically, and have typically been followed by the announcement of discoveries that exceed annual production, as a former Resources for the Future scholar, Bruce C. Netschert, steadily argued when it was not fashionable to do so.

8 'With a few notable exceptions, the most powerful influences on popular attitudes in upper-income countries – advertising and entertainment – promote over-consumption and waste.' *Caring for the Earth: A Strategy for Sustainable Living*, World Conservation Union, United Nations Environment Programme and the World Wide Fund for Nature, Gland, Switzerland, October 1991, p. 52. Hereinafter cited as *Caring for the Earth*. For a fuller and interesting discussion of advertising and its critics see John E. Calfee, *Fear of Persuasion: A New Perspective on Advertising and Regulation*, AEI Press, Washington, DC, 1997.

9 *Caring for the Earth*, p. 24.

10 Our burning of fossil fuels 'amounts to an addiction' that is 'bringing global environmental catastrophe'. The environmental ills consequent upon the use of fossil fuels 'are killing our water, our air, our plants, our animals, and eventually, if not checked, they will kill us.' Senator George J. Mitchell, *World on Fire: Saving an Endangered Earth*, Macmillan, New York, 1991, p. 47.

11 On this latter point see, for example, Alliance to Save Energy *et al.*, *America's Energy Choices: Investing in a Strong Economy and a Clean Environment*, Union of Concerned Scientists, Cambridge, MA, 1991, passim.

Consider, as one example of a reflexive antipathy to growth, then-Senator Al Gore's description of the construction of a large housing and shopping development in Virginia, one that would permit many families to realise the American dream of home ownership, create jobs and make life and shopping a bit easier. This construction is, to the Vice-President,[*] another example of 'human kind's assault on the earth ... As the woods fell to make way for more concrete, more buildings, parking lots, and streets, the wild things that lived there were forced to flee. Most of the deer were hit by cars ... '[12] No benefits of economic growth leapt to Gore's mind as he drove through Virginia; only costs.

This hostility to economic growth, and to the accompanying increase in material affluence, permeates much, although not all, environmentalist thinking. Consider the views of a prominent trio of environmental organisations. Convinced that 'economies and societies different from most that prevail today are needed if we are to care for the Earth [note: earth is often capitalised in environmental literature] and build a better quality of life for all',[13] these organisations contend, 'Affluence has not protected high-income countries or the wealthy minority in poor countries from drugs, alcoholism, AIDS, street violence and family breakdown.'[14] The fact that poverty hasn't done very much to eliminate these scourges remains unnoted, as have the facts that their incidence is considerably higher among the poor than among the affluent, and

---

[*]   Gore has rejoined the private sector, as a teacher of journalism at Columbia University.

12   Al Gore, *Earth in the Balance: Ecology and the Human Spirit*, Houghton Mifflin, Boston, 1992, p. 25.

13   *Caring for the Earth*, p. 1.

14   Ibid., p. 20.

that it is only the so-called 'high-income countries' that can afford to take effective measures against these ills. Rich remains better than poor, as every poor country knows.

This anti-growth bias of many environmentalists was, and to an extent that few will admit still is, matched by a pro-growth bias on the part of their opponents. Industry leaders, many of them remembering the days before World War II, when factories stood idle and the unemployed lined up at soup kitchens, thought it their duty to operate at full throttle, and to satisfy the desires of consumers for more and better products. To them, and to their successors, economic growth not only meant higher profits, but was and remains every bit as compelling a moral imperative as preservation of the environment was to the newly minted greens. To grow is to provide jobs, houses and the material things of life to consumers, dividends to investors, and national strength and prestige to America. There can be no higher calling.

Many industrialists quite correctly saw early efforts by environmentalists to persuade or, worse still, to force them to consider the environmental impacts of their production practices as an assault on these values, as a threat to their management prerogatives and to the profitability of their companies, and as part of an effort to undermine free markets and, indeed, capitalism itself. Their fears were fanned by the fact that early-day environmentalists often made common cause with opponents of capitalism and with other radical sorts with whom denizens of the nation's boardrooms did not communicate very well; these fears remain at high pitch today because businessmen believe that latter-day environmentalists are engaged in a relentless drive to pile regulation upon regulation, with no attention – indeed, a studied inattention – to the comparison of costs and benefits that businessmen favour.

But this devotion to cost-benefit analysis by most of industry comes late. Earlier in the debates, environmentalists pressing the quite sensible case that there might be certain external costs associated with the production techniques of modern industrial societies were not given much of a hearing. In part this was due to their willingness to jump from a demonstration that externalities exist to a call for regulation and/or taxes, a leap that Coase has shown is far from inevitable and, in the absence of high transactions or transition costs, most likely counterproductive.[15] But in part this unwillingness to give environmentalists a hearing was due to the quasi-religious fervour that many executives display when discussing economic growth. I well recall some of my friends in industry equating the smoke from factory stacks with prosperity – a charming anachronism, but an anachronism nonetheless. They were or chose to be unaware of the fact that their cries of laissez-faire had for centuries been raised 'as a defense of . . . vested interests who were imposing important external costs on society by unsanitary working and living conditions, child labor, pollution, etc.'.[16]

Please understand: you will find little overt anti-capitalist rhetoric emitting from today's environmentalists, and little overt green-bashing or pleas to be allowed to impose external costs on society in the public statements of today's public-relations-smoothed corprocrats. Political effectiveness goes not to the

15   R. H. Coase, 'The Problem of Social Cost', *Journal of Law and Economics*, vol. 3, October 1960, pp. 1–44, conveniently reprinted in *The Firm, the Market and the Law*, University of Chicago Press, Chicago, 1988, pp. 95–156.

16   Thomas Sowell, *Classical Economics Reconsidered*, Princeton University Press, Princeton, NJ, 1974, p. 30.

openly radical on either side, but to those who speak the language of compromise and concern.*

Besides, America's largest corporations are not insensitive to the fact that they are now well positioned to game the regulatory process, to the disadvantage of their smaller competitors and of potential new entrants. Anacharsis, a sixth-century Scythian prince, with what the *Oxford Classical Dictionary* describes as 'a high reputation for wisdom',[17] is believed to be the source of an observation cited by Jacob Viner: 'Laws are merely spider webs, which the birds, being larger, break through with ease, while the flies are caught fast.'[18] Had poor Anacharsis not been executed for his religious beliefs, he might have become a successful environmental lobbyist for some Fortune 500 company, devising regulations that would surely ensnare tiny flies, leaving his client-birds free to fly relatively unimpeded.

But be not misled by the more politic rhetoric of the combatants in the environmental policy arena: in the tussles that lie ahead, the old anti-growth and pro-growth prejudices lurk in the hearts of men, to paraphrase an old radio programme. To Al Gore's acolytes, more remains less. And to many of America's industrialists the notion of interfering with full employment, international competitiveness and the onward march of material progress seems a form of sacrilege, especially in a nation that is

---

* A possible exception is the travelling troupe of greenish anti-globalisation rioters, active first in Seattle, who seem to have cowed at least some politicians into reducing the enthusiasm of their support for freer trade.

17 Simon Hornblower and Antony Spawforth (eds), *The Oxford Classical Dictionary* (third edition), Oxford University Press, Oxford, 1996, p. 79.

18 See Jacob Viner, *Essays on the Intellectual History of Economics*, Douglas A. Irwin (ed.), Princeton University Press, Princeton, NJ, 1991, p. 289. Viner says that these words 'are attributed to Anacharsis'.

already spending $144 billion annually to comply with environmental regulations.[19]

Income distribution

Competing views of the desirability of economic growth and higher material standards of life are not the only deeply held visions that lurk beneath the surface of the debate over environmental policy. So, too, do views about the propriety of the income distribution system in this country and, indeed, in the world. The relatively recent contention by the Environmental Justice Movement that environmental degradation in America is concentrated in low-income and minority neighbourhoods is only the latest manifestation of the distributionist argument.[20]

On the international level, green groups argue that the industrialised world in general, and America in particular, consume a disproportionate amount of the world's resources and produce a disproportionate amount of its pollution. This usually takes the form of charging the US with consuming more oil and producing more pollution per capita than other countries,[21] as if some concept of fairness dictates that each person in the world is entitled to

---

19 Office of Management and Budget, Office of Information and Regulatory Affairs, *Report to Congress on the Costs and Benefits of Federal Regulations*, 30 September 1997, p. 29. These are 1996 dollars. The benefits are estimated at $162 billion (p. 33). Both figures are the subject of some controversy.

20 President Clinton, by Executive Order, established environmental justice as 'a national priority'. See Environmental Protection Agency, 'Environmental Justice', http://es.epa.gov/oeca/oejbut.html, 6 November 1997. See also the President's Memorandum for the Heads of All Departments and Agencies, http://www.epa.gov/docs/oejpubs/prezmemo.txt.html, 11 February 1994.

21 See, for example, National Academy of Sciences *et al.*, *Policy Implications of Greenhouse Warming*, National Academy Press, Washington, DC, 1991, p. 7.

an equal number of gallons of gasoline, and/or as if equal per capita shares were economically optimal. This egalitarianism-run-riot ignores the fact that America's energy-intensive agriculture feeds most of the world, that its huge distances compel the use of extensive trucking systems to distribute goods, and that its share of the world's output of CO_2 is in line with its share of the world's output of goods and services.

The redistributionist underpinnings of the environmental movement make discussions of problems that are genuinely international in character extraordinarily difficult because the proposed solutions are aimed at twin goals: protecting the environment, and redistributing the world's income. Thus, the World Wildlife Fund for Nature uses its website to encourage debate on the following topic: 'The rich must live more simply, so that the poor may simply live.' And on the question of whether sustainable development includes among its prerequisites 'the need for income redistribution'.[22]

The environmentalists' dissatisfaction with the way the world's income is distributed and its resources consumed comes face to face with the conviction on the part of many in American industry that incomes quite properly reflect marginal revenue product, that the earnings of working people (including themselves) are proportionate to their contributions to society, and that programmes that aim to take from the haves and give to the have-nots are likely to have unfortunate consequences, not least among them a reduction in the incentive for the world's most productive members to produce at full bore.

---

22 'Sustainable Development', http://www.panda.org/resources/factsheets/enviroecon/03sustdev.htm, 1993.

Thus, efforts to reduce Americans' consumption of resources so that more will somehow become available to poorer nations, which is what much of the new international environmental movement is all about, raise the hackles of those satisfied with the current distribution of income, and worry economists who fear that any disjunction between contribution to output and the reward for that contribution will inefficiently reduce total welfare.

It should be noted that the two issues we have been discussing – economic growth and income distribution – are not unrelated. Rapid growth has historically been accompanied by rising living standards for all groups, making economic growth perhaps the most successful of all anti-poverty programmes. As William Baumol and his colleagues point out, 'Rising incomes and the fruits of the technological revolution have filled our lives with goods and services unavailable, and even unimaginable, 100 years ago and, perhaps most important, the revolution has produced its most dramatic changes in the lives of the millions of ordinary working people.'[23] Indeed, although the benefits of this growth in the economy and in productivity were not distributed evenly, it is a fair conclusion that all income classes benefited: 'Even welfare recipients today are hardly expected to subsist on ... one bowl of gruel ... [and] the perpetual threat of famine ... has disappeared in this country and other industrialised lands. The end of that spectre is economic progress indeed, even for the poorest members of the community.'[24]

The conviction that economic growth, as we measure it, bene-

---

23 William J. Baumol, Sue Anne Batey Backman and Edward N. Wolff, *Productivity and American Leadership: the Long View*, MIT Press, Cambridge, MA, 1989, p. 57.

24 Ibid., pp. 58–9.

fits all groups makes it difficult for those who hold it to find common ground with proponents of programmes designed to reduce or even halt that growth in the interests of avoiding environmental degradation.

Government control of individual behaviour

The final factor making the environmental debate so heated is that it is merely a subset of a broader debate concerning the extent to which the government should be asked or allowed to interfere in the lives of its citizens. Many see regulations that require them to wear seat belts in their very own cars, not to smoke in their very own offices, to choose small over larger cars in response to taxes on the latter, to suffer the indignities of low-flow toilets, and not to keep guns in their very own homes, as intrusions on their personal liberty. Especially offensive are restrictions on the use or design of the automobile, which machine Americans quite properly see as providing the personal mobility that totalitarian regimes so fear.[25] Add urgings by assorted bureaucrats not to eat this or that food, or to boycott this or that toy that some child might decide to chew rather than cuddle, and you have in the minds of some a nanny state. Never mind even the most closely reasoned arguments about external costs and market failure: outside of the Beltway, freedom takes precedence.

Others contend that it is proper for government to look after the health of its citizens, if for no other reason than that some of the cost of unhealthful behaviour will fall on the public finances.

---

25 James D. Johnson, *Driving America: Your Car, Your Government, Your Choice*, AEI Press, Washington, DC, 1997, passim.

What to others seems an intrusion on individual choice is to regulatory activists the use of the resources and wisdom of government to channel people into the proper cars – or, better still, onto mass transit – or at least into HOV lanes on their highways and into health-food lanes in their supermarkets.

This conflict of visions comes to the fore as solutions to the alleged problem of global warming are mooted. As Linda Stuntz, a particularly thoughtful observer of the energy scene and a combatant in the environmental wars by virtue of her representation of a large coal-burning utility, recently pointed out, 'At least some adherents of the Politically Correct Energy Future ... are ready to expand the reach of government to impose unprecedented restrictions on our freedom. We all accept restrictions on our freedom every day to benefit the common good ... At some point, however, we need to ask ourselves whether these restrictions are truly worth the infringement on our liberty.'[26] And when we do, we can be certain that we will get wildly different answers from believers in the necessity of government intervention and from those more concerned with individual freedom of choice and action.

Interestingly, here we have a strange confluence of the views of activist environmentalists and social conservatives. The former *know* that it is better for us to ride on bicycles or use mass transit than to tool around in giant air-conditioned, gas-guzzling SUVs. They *know*, too, just how much glass an architect should be allowed to design into a house (the goal being to minimise fuel consumption for heating and cooling), and how many people should be allowed to visit our national parks. Social conservatives, sup-

---

26 'Global Warming and Energy Policy: Separating Fact from Fantasy', Presentation to the Center for Energy and Economic Development's Annual Board Meeting, 7 November 1997, p. 6 (mimeo).

posedly at the opposite end of the political spectrum from the environmentalists whom they tend to view as wreckers of the American economy, *know* which television programmes we should be allowed to watch, and which should be banned – I gather that old movies are 'in', but new sexy ones are 'out'; that Poirot is fine, but that *The Simpsons* is a threat to family values. (I believe, but am not certain, that it was Irving Kristol who first pointed out that liberals are opposed to showing violence on television, while conservatives are opposed to televised sex.)

In short, both environmentalists and social conservatives would substitute regulation, or as a second choice, in the case of environmentalists, taxes, for the market. Environmentalists have recently mounted an attack on the public's preference for big (safe) cars; social conservatives, or at least those not content with calling for voluntary, private-sector boycotts, continue to attempt to control television fare and Internet access. Little wonder that our Vice-President[*] finds both groups to his liking, granting the one all it desires by way of environmental restrictions, and the other approval for its efforts to dictate programming (more for kids, less for grown-ups), impose a government rating system on television networks, and supervise a 'voluntary' programme of controlled access to the Internet. We can only hope that he never seeks to satisfy both groups simultaneously, lest we be reduced to getting to the cineplex on our bicycles to find that we can see only *Mary Poppins* and *The Sound of Music*, while munching on unbuttered and unsalted popcorn.

The desire to limit individual choice, of course, is not a new phenomenon. And it is closely related to the notion that a steady

---

[*]   Al Gore, Vice-President at the time, no longer holds that office.

increase in the accumulation of material goods is somehow bad for us, and also threatens social harmony. This view has its roots in the sumptuary legislation that made its appearance as early as 594 BC. Those laws varied over time, but had in common restrictions on private consumption so as to prevent extravagance, preserve class distinctions in dress and entertainment, and preserve public morality.[27]

The assumption of these laws is that less is more, and that the state knows what is best for its citizens. They have their modern counterparts. One scholar, writing as early as 1934 – some sixty years before Hillary Clinton assumed responsibility for the nation's health – observed, 'Laws restraining and forbidding the use of liquor and tobacco have ... kinship with sumptuary legislation, for they are based upon the same principle, the protection of individual and public welfare and morality.'[28]

And before Hillary we had Jimmy – Carter, that is. He told us that '... too many of us now tend to worship self-indulgence and consumption ... But ... owning things and consuming things does not satisfy our longing for meaning ... [and] piling up material goods ... cannot fill the emptiness of lives which have no confidence or purpose.'[29]

From attitudes such as President Carter's and Mrs Clinton's it is an easy step to laws that tell us how fast we may drive, how cool

27 Sumptuary legislation was based on 'the feeling that luxury and extravagance were in themselves wicked and harmful to the morals of the people'. Frances Elizabeth Baldwin, *Sumptuary Legislation and Personal Regulations in England*, Johns Hopkins Press, Baltimore, MD, 1925, p. 10.

28 J . M. Vincent, 'Sumptuary Legislation', *Encyclopaedia of the Social Sciences*, vol. 14, Macmillan Group, New York, 1934, p. 466.

29 President Jimmy Carter, 'The Crisis of Confidence', Address to the Nation, 15 July 1979, p. 4 (mimeo).

and warm we may keep ourselves, how and of what materials we may build our houses, whether we may have frost-free refrigerators and self-cleaning ovens, whether we must join a car pool to have access to all the lanes of our tax-financed highways, how much water we may use to flush our toilets, and what fuels we may use to keep our lights on and our factories running.

As I pointed out earlier, a good portion of the usual crowd of conservative critics of environmental restrictions such as these come to this battle with unclean hands; since they have their own notions of the good life and of socially acceptable behaviour, and are willing to impose those notions on others, they are ill placed to argue that government impositions on individual freedom of choice are inadmissible. It is difficult to defend as God-given the right to drive a sports utility vehicle while puffing on a cigarette, while at the same time denying that people have a right to watch whatever television programme suits their fancy.

That leaves three groups that stand against the green machine of regulators and taxers: industry, free-market economists (who, of course, recognise the existence of external costs and market failure), and a cadre of multidisciplinary researchers dispassionately searching the data for guides to sensible policies – a group represented by our next speaker, Paul Portney, President of Resources for the Future.[30]

30 Libertarians might be counted a fourth group. But in this case they appear to be eligible for inclusion among the free-market economists, with whom they seem prepared to make common cause; witness the following from one of that group's intellectual leaders: 'The protection of the clean air has become an authentic public good, and under these circumstances [multiple polluters affecting multiple property owners] government legitimately acts as a forum for deciding how clean is clean enough and for crafting legislation to produce the desired result.' Charles Murray, *What It Means to Be a Libertarian*, Broadway Books, New York, 1997, p. 115.

Industrialists have some difficulty being heard because they are perceived to be acting out of self-interest and because the more powerful of them speak in muted tones,[31] both because they do not wish to alienate a possible future President [Al Gore, Vice-President at the time of this talk and correctly seen as the next Democratic candidate for President], and because they have confidence that they can survive any regulation that is aimed equally at their competitors.

That leaves two groups eligible for the battle: free-market economists, and multidisciplinary research teams rendered dispassionate by the benign environment of a well-ordered think tank. The latter, of course, include economists, and so these groups overlap. It will be well represented by our next speaker. I will speak only for free-market economists, with their kit of tools – prices, discount rates, costs, and cost-benefit analysis.

The best of the breed recognise two things: that markets are not perfect, and that their tools are not value-free. They also assume that it is worth the effort to quantify such benefits as the value of a hike in a national park and such costs as those associated with forgoing or sharply curtailing the use of fossil fuels. The more sensible keep in mind historian Eric Hobsbawm's observation that 'from time to time history catches economists at their brilliant gymnastics and walks off with their overcoats',[32] and so recognise that their quantification is not precise, but is best aimed at helping

---

31　There are honourable exceptions. See, for example, Lee Raymond's comments on the 'vast international bureaucracy responsible to no one' that Raymond contends would be required, along with 'punishing, high energy taxes', to achieve the reduction in carbon dioxide emissions that global warming advocates are seeking. Loc. cit.

32　Eric Hobsbawm, *On History*, The New Press, New York, 1997, p. 95.

policy-makers avoid the most egregious of the available errors.

But neither the fact that free-market economics represents a system of values, nor that a bit of humility is appropriate in applying the quantitative tools of the economist's trade, can be taken to mean that economists have little to offer in the debate over appropriate environmental policy. Indeed, there is no other group that can contribute as much. Environmentalists who decry the use of cost-benefit analysis are essentially asking for an open ticket to impose their vision of a good society on everyone else, and for a blank cheque with which to pay for that imposition.

For economists to be effective in promoting clear thinking, the limited goal set for them by John Maynard Keynes, they must first recognise that they are in a battle with opponents whose tactics have been beautifully described by Sowell. The key elements of these tactics are:

1. Assertions of a great danger to the whole society ...
2. An urgent need for action to avert impending catastrophe.
3. A need for government to drastically curtail the dangerous behaviour of the many, in response to the prescient conclusions of the few.
4. A disdainful dismissal of arguments to the contrary as either uninformed, or motivated by unworthy purposes.[33]

To many economists who inhabit campuses on which it invites ridicule to challenge the vision of the anointed, these tactics have proved intimidating: better to build huge, meaningless macroeconomic forecasting models that do not antagonise colleagues, but

---

33   Sowell, *Vision of the Anointed*, op. cit., p. 5.

do titillate the media, than to wrestle with controversial microeconomic issues,[34] particularly if one is of the view that the academic prejudice in favour of drastic government action (and more grants) is wrong.

For those who choose to do battle in the environmental arena, I can only advise the use of an assortment of weapons: a sense of humour when attacked as a philistine for defending the virtues of economic growth and rising material wellbeing; a sense of humility when offering conclusions based on quantitative assessments of difficult-to-measure phenomena; a recognition of the fact that market failure can occur, and warrant government action, even given the risk of regulatory failure; a realisation that the costs and benefits of policy changes should be measured by comparing, not some ideal circumstance, but the real-world present situation with the aimed-for new situation; an understanding that economics can inform policy judgements, but need not always supersede non-economic considerations;[35] and the conviction that rejection of the use of economic analysis will impoverish us materially, and deprive us of an anchor when the gales of special privilege hit the ship of state.

---

34 Why economists waste their time with forecasting is a mystery. 'The fact is economists are poor at forecasting short-term changes in the economy . . . Microeconomics attracts less attention from the media than does macroeconomics, yet it has had stunning practical successes during the past decade.' Gary S. and Guity Nashat Becker, *The Economics of Life*, McGraw Hill, New York, 1997, p. 311.

35 Amartya Sen is not alone in reminding us that 'modern economics [is] largely . . . an offshoot of ethics . . . The ethics-related tradition goes back at least to Aristotle.' *On Ethics & Economics*, Basil Blackwell, Oxford, 1987, p. 3.

Energy markets or energy policy: which way prosperity?

*The following remarks were delivered at the Royal Society for the En-
couragement of Arts, Manufacture and Commerce on 28 February
2000 as part of the Cantor Lecture Series on Energy and Society. The
theme of the talk is that markets make more efficient decisions than do
regulators and politicians, but that in the absence of effectively competitive markets and economically accurate prices, regulation is required to
prevent monopolistic exploitation. A sub-theme is that energy policy is
inextricably intertwined with environmental policy.*

Mr Chairman, ladies and gentleman.

The title of this talk, 'Energy Markets or Energy Policy: Which
way Prosperity?', was crafted to permit me to discuss with you this
evening the question of whether markets or men should be the
primary instruments on which we rely to produce energy prices
that maximise the efficiency with which the world's energy resources are used. So as to avoid holding those of you who are unfa-
miliar with my views in intolerable suspense, I will give you the
answer now, and then proceed to defend it. I would prefer to see
resources allocated by markets rather than by ministers. But the
special characteristics of energy markets – most notably the tendency towards cartels or monopoly in some segments, and the impact of energy production and consumption on the environment –
require careful attention to the structure of those markets, and to
the economic content of the prices prevailing in those markets.

Policy lurches

Some ten years ago, when asked to participate in an energy policy
conference at the University of Surrey, I said that an energy policy-

maker is very unlike a bachelor. A bachelor, it is said, is a man who never makes the same mistake once. An energy policy-maker, by contrast, is a person who, if permitted to do so, will willingly repeat past errors and tirelessly invent new ones.[36]

As the IEA's Professor Colin Robinson has pointed out, much of what passes for energy policy is a 'haphazard process of piling measure on measure' in response to perceived emergencies, often followed by a White Paper attempting to make *ad hoc*-ery seem a considered judgement based on careful analysis.[37] Thus, in America, our politicians, having only a few months ago urged Saudi Arabia to raise the price of crude oil so as to shore up a regime perceived as friendly to United States' interests, and not incidentally to put a bit more revenue into the pockets of domestic oil producers, are now scrambling to get the Saudis and their cartel partners to increase production so as to lower crude oil prices, lest the prosperity of the trucking, airline and hotel industries (the latter depends heavily on summer drivers) be threatened and, possibly, the current economic boom aborted.

These lurches are quite typical when politicians confront problems in energy markets. But they at least have the virtue of being short-lived. The greater danger occurs when policy-makers actually take the time and trouble to develop long-run energy policies, for their errors then prove less reversible once they are enshrined in legislation or in regulations governing prices, supply and demand.

---

36 'A Market-based Energy Policy: The Alternative to Past Errors', in Peter Pearson (ed.), *Energy Policies in an Uncertain World*, Macmillan Press, London, 1989, p. 44. The outline of issues presented in that paper remains relevant today, and has been drawn on here.

37 See his 'Energy Policy: Errors, Illusions and Market Realities', Occasional Paper 90, Institute of Economic Affairs, London, 1993, p. 14.

Long-run policy

Typically, energy policy-making begins with a forecast of demand and supply. These forecasts typically produce one of three results:

1. Supply will fall short of demand, producing a 'shortage'.
2. Supply will be adequate to satisfy demand, but only because demand is satisfied in a manner somehow unacceptable to the policy-maker.
3. Supply and demand will be in balance, but at prices deemed by the policy-maker to be unacceptable politically – either so high as to outrage consumers, or so low as to outrage producers.

The first, or shortage, case results when demand is predicted to grow at some steady pace, while the energy resource base from which that demand will be met is taken as finite, and the technology affecting costs and availability are assumed to be frozen at present levels. The predicted shortfall justifies intervening in markets (although, as I shall point out in a moment, finding themselves short of a shortfall, they will make do with a glut). That is why Congressman Dick Armey (Republican, Texas) has warned, 'Never trust pessimistic forecasts from people who make a living selling government.'[38]

In the second case – the one in which demand can be satisfied, but only by drawing on 'unacceptable' sources of energy – the justifications for intervention may be environmental concerns (more renewables), or social concerns (preserve miners' jobs), or security concerns (fear of excessive reliance on imports).

---

38   Quoted in *Forbes*, 25 March 1996, p. 30.

In the third case – 'unacceptable' prices required to balance demand and supply – the justifications for intervention are, alternately, the plight of consumers (read 'voters') hard pressed by high prices, or of producers (read 'voting blocs') oppressed by low prices.

Faced with these concerns, the policy-maker will wield the tools of his trade with abandon. Let me refresh your recollection as to the character of three of those tools:

1. One such is the subsidy, deployed to encourage the production of some energy source that is the choice *du jour* of the policy-maker.
2. Another is taxation, deployed to discourage use of energy in general, or reliance on the energy source currently in disfavour.
3. A third, which makes its appearance when supply and demand can be balanced only at prices politicians deem unacceptable, is income redistribution, achieved overtly by grants to favoured consumers, sometimes but not always the poor, sometimes the merely old, be they rich or poor; or covertly, by having the regulators offer preferential treatment to some class of customer that catches the eye of the politician as elections approach.

Thus, we have subsidies for so-called 'renewable' energy sources in your country and mine, and for coal in yours; taxes on energy consumption, again in your country and mine, although your officials have carried these taxes to extremes that would be politically unacceptable in mine; grants to Americans who find it more expensive to heat their homes this winter than last, and to

British pensioners; and, in both of our countries, discount prices for electricity and gas for consumers determined by ministers, Congressmen or regulators to be worthy of special attention.

Reasons for special concern with energy

Why all of this intervention in energy markets? There are many reasons, of which I will cite six:

1. The energy industries are typically important components of a nation's GDP, and of its investment infrastructure. In developing countries, these industries are often the bottleneck that must be broken if overall economic development is to proceed.
2. The energy industries directly affect more consumers than any other: everyone drives petrol-fuelled vehicles, heats his or her home with oil, gas or electricity; relies on electricity for light and cooling; and is increasingly aware of the importance of quality electric service to prevent blinking clocks on video machines and crashes of computers.
3. The energy industries have a major impact on the quality of the environment.
4. Many components of the energy industry possess strong cartel or monopoly characteristics.
5. The industries are going through a major restructuring: consolidation in the oil industry which interests competition authorities, especially the Federal Trade Commission in America; and deregulation in the gas and electric industries, a process that attracts legislators and regulators in the countries in which those processes are under way.

6. Finally, there is something – and I am not sure just what – about the oil industry that attracts the attention of policy-makers, both in consuming and in producing nations. On the consumer side of the pump there is concern with security of supply, and price spikes; on the producing side, oil is often the principal source of a nation's revenues and in Arab countries is regarded as 'the blood of the earth', or, as with Mexico, somehow seen as part of that nation's *patrimonio*, to be treated differently from other goods offered on world markets, and deserving of very special consideration when public policy is to be made.

Bases for intervention

On a more general level, there are three propositions that seem to be the basis for government intervention in energy markets:

1. Policy-makers often talk the talk of free markets, but less often walk the walk. They just do not think it proper to allow impersonal market forces (i.e. something independent of themselves) to decide who shall consume what fuels, in what quantities and at what prices. This antipathy to free markets stems from two assumptions.

(i.) The first is that the distribution of income, which in turn determines the ability to purchase energy, is in some sense unfair. Accepting price as an allocative tool means accepting the current distribution of income as determinative of who shall be able to command which goods. That, politicians are rarely willing to do – a reluctance confined not only to the energy industries, but evident as well in the healthcare sector. Energy policy, therefore, is designed to introduce some alternative to price as an allocative tool (queuing, in the case of gasoline during supply interruptions in America, analogous to the method of handling shortages of healthcare facilities in Britain), or some redistribution of income from higher to lower earners, specifically earmarked for energy purchases.

This inclination by many policy-makers to reject the way that markets distribute income applies not only within countries, but internationally. It was on display here last week, during Professor Hogan's lecture, when our good chairman bemoaned the fact that Americans drive large, safe, comfortable cars,[39] and cheerfully buy gasoline in huge quantities at prices that do not include taxes of the sort that all of your political parties agree should be extracted from motorists.

Thus, those of my American friends who visit this country and the Continent less frequently than I do are always amazed at the pervasiveness of this view that America somehow consumes 'too much' of the world's energy resources, as if some equal per capita consumption of the world's energy resources would be more 'just' than greater use by more productive economies, and as if these resources did not exist in ample supply to meet the needs of all of the world's consumers as far ahead as the eye can see.

(ii.) The second reason that policy-makers are unfond of free

---

39 There can be no doubt that bigger cars are safer than smaller cars. 'Studies . . . show that when two smaller cars of equal weight crash head-on at equal speed, the risk of driver death or injury is about twice as great as when two cars, each twice as heavy as the first cars, experience the same type of crash.' See Johnson, op. cit., p. 25.

markets is that prices sometimes go up, on occasion quite sharply, causing an outbreak of the disease that politicians fear most – voter anger. In Britain, electricity prices spiked in the summer of 1999, producing a legislative-regulatory reaction that I will discuss later in this talk; in America the same phenomenon raised serious questions in the minds of some as to the desirability of continuing down the road to deregulation. And of course this winter's rise in heating oil and gasoline prices has America's politicians calling for action ranging from the sale of oil from the Strategic Petroleum Reserve to the jaw-boning of Saudi Arabia and Kuwait – within recent American (although not Saudi or Kuwaiti) memory saved from conquest by Saddam Hussein – to persuade them to open their taps a bit wider.

These price incidents, politicians feel, threaten their tenure in office. So rather than let prices rise to balance demand and supply, they intervene, with something they like to call an energy policy.

2. The second major element reflected in most energy policy exercises is what I would call the sumptuary mentality.

The historians among you will recall that the people of the Middle Ages believed that government had every right to enact sumptuary laws that restrained extravagance by individuals,[40] the theory being that 'luxury and extravagance were in themselves wicked and harmful to the morals of the people'.[41] That this notion should appeal to today's politicians should come as no surprise. We in America had our bout with President Jimmy Carter, who told us that '... too many of us now tend to worship self-

---

40   Baldwin, op. cit., p. 9.
41   Ibid, p. 10.

indulgence and consumption ... Piling up material goods cannot fill the emptiness of lives which have no confidence or purpose.'[42] This justified ruling out the use of fuels to heat water in public places such as airports, and still other regulations as to permissible thermostat settings in summer and winter. Our then-President felt that being warm in winter and cool in summer would somehow damage our souls.

In your country, the sumptuary mentality permeates the thinking of ministers who drive rather than walk short distances to podia from which to exhort citizens to walk rather than drive, who feel that one house is all that a non-ministerial person really needs, and who set taxes designed to confine non-ministers to small, unsafe but fuel-saving automobiles.

It is this sumptuary mentality which gives energy policy-makers leave to intervene in markets to prevent 'wasteful' or 'excessive' use of energy. So we have environmentalists in my country who oppose the use of self-cleaning ovens, or self-defrosting refrigerators, on the grounds that it is somehow bad for us to avoid the cleaning and defrosting chores that will make better men and women of us all.

3. The third attitude that underlies much of energy policy-making might best be termed an anti-risk attitude. This desire of politicians to invent a risk-free society is, of course, not peculiar to the energy industries. We see it in attempts to regulate medical research and to delay or prevent the introduction of new drugs and more productive agricultural techniques; in efforts by the cigarette police to tell otherwise free citizens how to balance the risks and

42   Address to the Nation, 15 July 1979, p. 4 (mimeo).

pleasures of smoking; in government rules that prevented the eating of beef on the bone, lest the consumer add to the risk that he will be struck by lightning during his meal.

In short, our elected and appointed officials seem to feel – and I know not whether they are correct in this – that voters want a society in which innovation is subordinated to safety, progress to risk aversion. In the case of energy policy in our countries and in Europe, this takes the form of eliminating nuclear power as one of the sources of electrical energy; of preventing pipeline access to remote regions in which gas and oil exist, alongside caribou; and of requiring the installation of equipment at costs far in excess of the benefits to be obtained.[*]

My view – and I assume we will have a conversation about this later this evening – is that these three forces that shape energy policy lead to inefficiencies and muddle. The lack of faith in markets leads to meddling which produces inefficiencies that we can ill afford; the sumptuary mentality gives policy-makers licence to impose their values on everyone save themselves; and the anti-risk attitude deprives society of innovations that it needs if productivity is to continue to provide an impetus to continued inflation-free economic growth.

---

[*] In a reversal of US policy, President George W. Bush and Vice-President Richard Cheney propose to open a portion of the Alaskan reserve to oil and gas drilling, and to revive the nuclear industry by reforming licensing procedures and continuing to subsidise nuclear plant operators by limiting their liability in the case of catastrophic accidents. It is far from certain that Congress will approve these initiatives.

Use of demand forecasts

But the dangerous nature of the underpinnings of what has passed for energy policy is not the only reason for preferring markets to ministers. The other is that energy policy, based as it inevitably is on forecasts of demand and supply, becomes enshrined in directives, policy papers and legislation. Even when free from political influence, these forecasts are at best imperfect, at worst wildly off the mark. Econometric techniques cannot be adapted to oil markets that are dominated by a producer cartel; advances in technology have regularly knocked forecasts of future production costs into a cocked hat; and energy markets are more sensitive than most to political shocks such as the Gulf War.[43]

It is true, of course, that managers of our energy companies also rely on forecasts. But when these forecasts prove wrong, they receive a short, sharp smack on their bottom lines. And they adjust, or they perish. Laws, ministerial directives and regulatory decisions, by contrast, change only slowly in response to the unexpected.

Anyone who has been involved in trying to change healthcare policy to accommodate the increase in longevity made possible by new medical technologies, or telecoms policy to accommodate the emergence of the Internet as a force to be reckoned with, or aviation policy to make possible increased competition at Heathrow, will know that policy changes at a glacial place even though market conditions now change at the speed of light.

---

43 Some of the changes that it is difficult for any model to accommodate are mentioned, although not in that context, in the report of the 1999 Aspen Energy Policy Forum, 'Fuel Choice, Supply, and Reliability in the 21st Century'. They include the restructuring of the electric industry, the competition of new technologies and new fuels for markets, changes in environmental policy, and 'new technologies that may lead to vastly different vehicle/fuels power plants' (pp. 10ff.).

So in the end we must rely on the market, rather than on government-crafted policies, if we are to have an ample supply of energy at efficient prices. But for the market to work properly, the price signals it sends must meet two criteria: they must be set at competitive levels, and they must reflect *all* of the costs associated with the production and use of the energy source in question.

The role of competition and regulation

Let me treat the question of competition first. One need not be an expert in energy markets to know that there are major elements of monopoly present in these energy markets.

Start with the price of oil. Whatever we might think about the long-run viability of a cartel – and my view is that in the long run the development of new sources of supply, new technologies and cheating by cartel members will constrain the power of any such conspiracy – there is no question that over the medium term the OPEC cartel can keep prices far above competitive levels.

And I have reference to more than the cartel's current success in keeping prices close to $30 per barrel – with the help, of course, of Mexico, which is not an OPEC member but which brokered the deal between Venezuela and Saudi Arabia that has caused the current run-up in prices.[44] The best available estimate is that the cost

44 Both Venezuela and Saudi Arabia feared that if they cut back production, Mexico (not an OPEC member) would capture a greater share of the US market. When Mexico agreed to co-operate with the cartel by not filling any gaps created by OPEC's production cuts, the deal was struck that sent prices soaring. It is a testimonial to the ineptitude of US foreign policy-makers that this assault on American prosperity is being perpetrated by one country that depends on America to defend it from invasion (Saudi Arabia), and another (Mexico) that depends for its prosperity on the NAFTA free trade agreement and for its social stability on America's willingness to turn a blind eye to the illegal immigrants it exports to the US.

of finding a new barrel of oil in the Middle East is 'much below' $3 per barrel, and the cost of producing it $2 per barrel at the very most.[45] This means that even at the allegedly depressed price of $10 per barrel, oil was selling at substantially above the price that would prevail in a competitive market.

Like oil, but for different reasons, gas and electricity are not sold in fully competitive markets. Although substantial progress has been made in your country and mine in deregulating the generation segment of the electricity industry, and the production segment of the gas industry, the delivery systems remain, at least for now, monopolies. And both fuels have environmental costs and benefits that must be reckoned with in formulating a proper energy policy, a chore to which I now turn.

The role of efficient prices

The basis for any such policy must be an effort to get prices right, by which I mean setting rules that result in prices set at competitive levels, and internalising all of the external costs of production and consumption. Let me offer a few suggestions.

(i) Oil

In the case of oil, a commodity intermittently dominated by a cartel, America can lead the way by making certain that the price paid by consumers includes all of the external costs associated with the use of imported oil. Most notable among those external

---

45   Nader A. Sultan, Deputy Chairman, Kuwait Petroleum Corporation, in 'Energy After 2000', a report of the VIII Repsol-Harvard Seminar, held in Seville, Spain, June 1997, pp. 129–30.

costs are the risks associated with relying on imports from countries that vary between the unstable and the overtly hostile. But some of these costs are not reflected in the price paid for oil by consumers, most notably the macroeconomic risks necessarily associated with price spikes and supply cut-offs that seem to accompany reliance on imported oil, and the costs when those risks are realised.

Given that fact, a policy should be adopted that includes taxation of imports to finance (a) an adequate strategic petroleum reserve,[46] (b) the costs of supply diversity if non-OPEC sources prove more costly than supplies from the cartel, and (c) the costs of developing alternatives to the use of imported oil, including conservation devices and techniques.

But the existence of external costs associated with the use of imported oil is not a licence for policy-makers to ignore sensible economics. The need to internalise these costs cannot be an excuse for:

- adopting this or that pet technology of some vote-starved Iowa politician – note that only Senator John McCain, among a field then consisting of more than a half-dozen presidential candidates from both parties, refused to promise Iowa voters that, if elected, he would continue the ridiculously costly programme of converting corn into motor fuel;
- pandering to some Old Labour romantic who remembers (or

---

46 Note that I did not say *the* Strategic Petroleum Reserve, which is nothing more than 567 million barrels of oil buried in salt domes, and in search of a policy to dictate the circumstances under which they will be used.

was told of) the glory of going miles under the earth to wrest from it a meagre and distinctly unhealthy living;

- being too embarrassed to oppose some over-zealous environmentalist to whom cost is no object.

Instead, we must adhere to a principle that is simple in concept although difficult in application. In a brief essay, Paul Portney, the President of Resources for the Future, a non-partisan and highly respected think tank in Washington, set out what he called 'a model of environmental decision making in … the rationalist mode', a model that applies to the treatment of all external costs. What Portney calls the 'first element, or principle' of that approach 'is that we ought to balance the incremental benefits of a proposed policy change with incremental costs at the margin'. Recognising that quantification is often difficult, Portney suggests that this first principle be applied either 'qualitatively or quantitatively', for even the qualitative approach will provide a framework within which the right question can be asked: does this policy promise to do more good than harm?[47]

In America, the provisional answer seems to be that a non-policy towards oil imports, or reliance on episodic jaw-boning, promises to do more harm than one that would attempt to impose the external costs of oil consumption on consumers. At the risk of disappointing you, I should add that this does not mean loading all of the costs on petrol, or of raising petrol taxes to anything like the levels to which you are accustomed here: those are designed to

---

47 Paul Portney, 'A Rationalist Program for Environmental Policy Making', in *Making Environmental Policy*, American Enterprise Institute, Washington, DC, 1998, pp. 21–9.

be punitive, and to generate revenues for the Chancellor, rather than to internalise any as yet uninternalised cost.[48]

(ii) Electricity

Electricity prices present a case conceptually similar to that of oil: they are not set in effectively competitive markets, and we have to consider the externalities, in this case the environmental impact of electricity production and use. Start with competition.

It seems safe to assume that competition for customers by suppliers is reasonably effective. True, incumbents have the advantage of brand identification and consumer inertia. True, too, some of the sales tactics used by various competitors seem excessively robust, especially to English sensibilities. But customers now have a realistic opportunity to switch suppliers, and the fact that many have chosen not to do so is irrelevant, despite the tendency of many regulators to define competition in terms of how many customers have chosen to exercise their new freedom.[49] Of course, incumbents that use tactics designed to bar access and entry to

---

48 Energy taxes seem to be an attractive source of revenues for European politicians. Maria Teresa Estevan Bolea, at the time a member of the European Parliament, recently told a gathering of energy industry executives and policy-makers, 'You should not expect energy taxes to decrease – they won't ... With a large aging population, requiring enormous costs in pensions and related expenses, where can the money come from? From a splendid product, with a rigid demand curve ... gasoline.' In William Hogan and Irwin M. Stelzer (eds), 'Preparing for the Twenty-First Century', a report of the X Repsol-Harvard Seminar on Energy Policy, Madrid, June 1999, p. 149.

49 In fact it is difficult to see what is worrying the Minister of Trade and Industry about the switch rate. PowerGen, for example, lost 200,000 of its approximately 2.5 million retail customers within two months of the opening of the electricity market in May 1999. *Financial Times*, 23 February 2000.

newcomers should be dealt with swiftly and severely, either by regulatory or by competition authorities.

What we do have to worry about is whether the prices set in the generation market are competitively determined, and how to set prices for the use of monopoly wires. All of this, of course, is the subject of legislation now wending its way through Parliament to increase the sway of regulation in UK electricity markets, and of policies being promulgated in my country by the Federal Energy Regulatory Commission.

That new regulatory tools are necessary there can be little doubt. I say that with some reluctance, because I agree with Sir Bryan Carsberg that regulation should be instituted only after a clear case has been made that competition is inadequately strong to protect consumers:

> ... promoting competition is often a better approach than detailed regulation. Detailed regulation depends for its success on the ability of one or a few people to judge what is best for consumers. Regulators exercise this judgement imperfectly. Market competition is usually better partly because of its ability to surprise. Its results may well outstrip the daring of even the boldest regulator.[50]

The hard fact is that no matter how talented the regulator, the very process of regulation is a highly imperfect instrument, more imperfect even than imperfectly competitive markets in producing an efficient use of resources. As one of the leading texts in the field puts it:

---

50 Sir Bryan Carsberg, 'Competition Regulation the British Way: Jaguar or Dinosaur?', Occasional Paper 97, Institute of Economic Affairs, London, p. 9. Originally the Twenty-Fifth Wincott Memorial Lecture delivered at the Institution of Mechanical Engineers, Westminster, 20 November 1995.

> ... the many difficulties inherent in regulation [include]
> only partially observable efficiency, superior information
> possessed by the regulated enterprise ... , and the incentives
> for strategic behaviour inherent in periodic regulatory
> reviews ... Overall, regulation ... is far from being a full
> substitute for competition, it can create systematic
> distortions, it generally faces a trade-off between promoting
> one type of efficiency at the expense of another, and it is
> likely to generate significant costs, in terms of both direct
> implementation and exacerbation of inefficiency.[51]

But in the absence of effective competition, regulation – with all of its frailties – becomes a necessity. And to understand the turn that regulation has now taken in Britain it is important to understand that New Labour, for all its bows in the direction of Lady Thatcher's achievements, never had any intention of being bound by the regulatory and environmental policies she enacted to govern the new private-sector companies. Tony Blair believes government can make things better; Lady Thatcher believes that government often makes things worse. He believes utilities have a right to fair profits and no more; Lady Thatcher rarely saw a profit margin that she felt was too high.

You will recall that the immediate post-privatisation era was characterised by what was known as 'light-handed regulation'. Such a regime appealed to the Thatcher government because the goal of the privatisation process was to create a nation of small shareholders, with political interests opposed to those of the then-powerful trade unions. The hope was that minimal regulation of

---

51 Donald A. Hay and Derek J. Morris, *Industrial Economics and Organization: Theory and Evidence*, Oxford University Press, Oxford, 1991, pp. 636–7.

the electric, gas and other privatised companies would produce profits that would drive share prices steadily higher, persuading small investors of the virtues of share ownership.

That hope was realised – too fully to be politically sustainable. Returns on equity began to exceed 20 per cent; utility executives who had never in their lives received a call from a headhunter became persuaded that they were hot properties who must be made instant millionaires lest they flee to other countries to mismanage utilities there; the pricing system on the electric grid proved to be subject to manipulation by the generating duopoly; and the regulators attempting to control prices and standards of service in the gas industry proved no match for a vertically integrated monopoly with huge resources and control of the information that is the stuff of day-to-day regulation.

This made the energy utilities a plump target for a Labour Party desperately in need of revenues, it having promised not to raise income tax rates in order to persuade the electorate that it was no longer a tax-and-spend party. So it levied a one-time 'windfall profits tax' on the utilities, with the proceeds to be used to fund a scheme for reducing teenage unemployment.

More important, New Labour Party policy-makers discovered that Old Labour's dream of controlling the commanding heights of the economy did not mean that one must take those industries into the public sector. Instead, the government could accomplish its goals by regulation – a cheap but effective way of bending the energy utilities to New Labour's will.

New Labour had, and has, several goals. One was to introduce competition as quickly as possible, which it has more or less accomplished. In the generation sector, concentration has been sharply reduced, with the combined share of PowerGen and

National Power reduced from 80 per cent to 20 per cent, in part as a result of the construction of new plant, in part as the result of Mission Energy's purchase of Ferrybridge (1,994 megawatts) and Fiddler's Ferry (1,960 megawatts) from PowerGen. Unfortunately, in order to induce divestitures by the duopolists, the government felt it necessary to permit some vertical reintegration; that will surely create regulatory problems in the future.

At the retail level, Labour has kept its pledge to see to it that every consumer in Britain has a free choice of gas and electric suppliers,[52] although its Trade and Industry Secretary is unhappy that 80 per cent of customers have decided not to switch suppliers and, like his counterparts in the American regulatory community, mistakenly takes this to mean that competition is not working.

A second goal of New Labour was to put some downward pressure on utility rates and on profit margins – to replace what it saw as overly permissive regulation, and the regulators it perceived as overly generous, with stricter rules and harder men. (If one were permitted a pun, one might say that New Labour has a tendency to prefer more militant regulators – a sort of Militant Tendency.) That, too, New Labour has accomplished. Stephen Littlechild has been replaced as electric regulator by Callum McCarthy, an economist of less academic bent and more interested in leavening economic considerations with a yeasty dose of political and social factors. He has already made his mark by ordering major rate cuts, and by proposing to change the licences under which generators operate so as to include 'good market behaviour' clauses that will

---

52   Utilities have found wooing customers by door-to-door selling to be expensive. Eastern Group, owned by Texas Utilities, estimates that it costs £30 to sign up a customer, and that it takes two years to move into profit on a new customer. *Financial Times*, 11 June 1999.

give him the power to levy unlimited fines if, in defiance of his order, the companies engage in 'opportunistic behaviour' or 'damaging opportunism'.[53] This comes at a time when the generating market is becoming more competitive; a liquid, efficient contract market is starting to develop; and a new Competition Act has been passed which already contains provisions that guard against anti-competitive behaviour, all of which suggest that a tightening of regulation is unnecessary.

But the regulator's action, and the government's plan to support his actions with legislation – what the US trade press characterises as 'a touch of re-regulation in an era of deregulation'[54] – is not totally unreasonable. In the case of generation, the pool apparently did not work well, especially in the summer of 1999;[55] and manipulation by some generators of capacity availability and hence of prices was not unknown. It is certainly arguable that competition policy, which bases most of its actions on a prior finding of market dominance, cannot cope with a situation in which short-term inelasticities of supply and demand present firms that do not have a dominant position, as that phenomenon is conventionally understood, with an opportunity for price manipulation.

In the case of the wires business, the post-Thatcher era of regulation has been marked by an attempt to use intercompany cost comparisons to drive all players towards the standards set by those who seem to be the most efficient operators. The difficulties

---

53 The Office of Gas and Electricity Markets, 'The New Electricity Trading Arrangements and Related Transmission Issues. Proposals on Licence Changes. A Consultative Document', December 1999, pp. 29–30. (Such clauses have since been stricken down by the Competition Commission, to which some utilities appealed for relief.)

54 The Electricity Daily, 31 January 2000.

55 Ibid.

in estimating the economic cost of providing utility services have been laid out by Alfred Kahn in his classic study of utility regulation,[56] the flaws in using such comparisons to set utility prices have been well documented elsewhere,[57] and any fair reading of the reports of Ofgem leads to the conclusion that there is as much art as science in that agency's conclusions as to the appropriate level of wires charges.

But the process of regulation in Great Britain must be viewed as still evolving. Once Ofgem has succeeded in establishing a uniform system of accounts so that it can analyse costs on a common basis, its efforts to use intercompany cost comparisons may well improve sufficiently to increase the ratio of science to art in its determinations. And it is possible – although American investors, accustomed as they are to constitutional protections and due process, will take some convincing – that a dollop of good British common sense will be used to dilute in practice the unlimited powers that the Director-General of Ofgem will have in law.

Indeed, many of us who have found the measurement of management performance in monopoly utilities most difficult are looking forward to the Director-General's findings under the provision that requires him to link directors' pay to quality of service. And we are eager to learn, too, just how to distinguish price rises at peak times that are legitimate responses to supply-demand imbalances from the forbidden 'opportunistic behaviour'. Mr McCarthy

---

56 These difficulties are described in connection with the computation of marginal costs, but are applicable in this context as well. Alfred E. Kahn, *The Economics of Regulation: Principles and Institutions*, vol. 1, John Wiley & Sons, Inc., New York, 1970, pp. 70ff.

57 William B. Shew, 'Yardstick Competition and the Regulation of Natural Monopoly', *Essays in Regulatory Policy*, Hudson Institute, Indianapolis, IN, 1999.

has an opportunity for intellectual breakthroughs that have eluded many of us for more years than I care to remember!

Meanwhile, until they see how the provisions of the new law are applied, investors and utility managers will have to live with increased uncertainty and regulatory risk.

The role of environmental costs

If regulation is got right, the remaining chore in crafting a sensible, market-based energy policy will be to make certain that energy prices incorporate all of the costs imposed on society by consumers and producers. I have already discussed the possible need for changes in American policy towards oil imports, so as to reflect such costs associated with the risk of supply interruptions and price spikes as are not yet included in prices.

Let me turn now to the UK, and the relation of environmental to energy policy.

Here all seems to be a muddle, with some policies aimed at cleaning the air, others certain to foul it. New Labour, for all its modernising tendencies, is, after all, still a Labour Party. And the heart of the party remains committed to the dwindling band of coal miners that still extracts some very expensive and dirty coal from Britain's remaining mines. When the electric utility contracts to buy this coal expired, and it looked as though some of the last few mines would close as natural gas replaced coal (or that 'the country could effectively lose a meaningful coal option', to use the more obscure formulation used in the government's report on the subject[58]), Labour found itself torn between its non-

---

58 Department of Trade and Industry, 'Review of Energy Sources for Power Generation', Consultation Document, 25 June 1998.

interventionist speeches and its historic attachment to the coal miners who were once the core of the party, and whose thuggish union Margaret Thatcher had faced down.

History won. The government declared a – dubbed by it 'a stricter consents policy' – on the construction of new gas-fired power plants.[*] This despite the fact that most studies show that such a policy destroys more jobs than it creates. Old Labour politicians quite unashamedly confessed – no, boasted – that the decision to slow 'the dash for gas' was designed to preserve miners' jobs. New Labour politicians, aware that this action contradicted their reformist rhetoric and would antagonise the Middle England greens whom they are wooing, had to find other reasons for interfering in an energy market that has decided that new gas-fired plants are more efficient than old coal-fired stations that rely on UK coal.

A politician in search of a rationalisation is rarely frustrated in his hunt. New Labour ministers discovered two justifications for intervention: that the wholesale market for electricity is biased in favour of gas and against coal, and that it is important to preserve diversity and security of supply of fuel sources.

Whatever the truth of the first of these allegations at the time it was made – that the electric market is rigged in favour of gas – it is no longer true, as I believe Ofgem has pointed out. But the restrictions remain, proving two points that I made earlier: policy changes more slowly than markets, and history often trumps economics.

As for the second point – that coal provides security of electricity supply – those who remember the days when the coal min-

---

[*]   That moratorium has been allowed to expire.

ers held the nation to ransom by denying it the fuel on which 80 per cent of its electricity generating capacity then relied must be permitted a wry smile. But New Labour ministers kept a straight face, and used diversity and security as the basis for supporting the moratorium without surrendering their New Labour market-bought clothes.

The stricter consents policy has denied or delayed planning consents to gas plants with a total capacity of 5,800 megawatts, and turned away almost £3 billion of capital investment that would provide many more jobs, albeit some of them of only two to three years' duration during the construction phase, than there are coal miners. And the coal miners' jobs are dirty, dangerous and in the long run doomed.

A policy of subsidising the production of the dirtiest of all fuels, and repressing the use of perhaps the cleanest, is of course inconsistent with Britain's desire to lead the world in reducing greenhouse gas emissions, and with the new Act's imposition of financial penalties on suppliers that do not purchase renewable energy in quantities judged by the minister to be sufficient. It is also wildly inconsistent with a climate change levy, which studies now show would be unnecessary to meet the government's environmental targets if even one-third of the fifteen gas-fired stations denied permits under the moratorium had been built and operated at their normal 80 per cent load factors.[59]

Any policy aimed at preventing climate change, of course, must be developed with an eye to the following facts:

---

59 *Financial Times*, 23 February 2000, reporting comments by Helen Liddell, the energy minister, and a study by the House of Commons library.

- the science of global warming is sufficiently uncertain to warrant caution in adopting costly policies to combat it, but sufficiently suggestive to justify sensible steps to combat it;[60]
- money available for environmental enhancement might be better spent on subsidising clean water and sewage systems;[61]
- the international institutional arrangements that will be necessary to the efficient implementation of a policy designed to combat global warming will be exceedingly difficult, if not impossible, to develop;[62] and
- a warmer globe may harm some, but it will benefit others. It might, for example, actually benefit Blackpool while damaging Cannes, and, if scientists at the Environmental Change Institute at Oxford are correct, enable the south of England to overtake France as the principal producer of white wines, and give lovers of claret the opportunity to quaff Cabernet Canterbury and Maison Maidstone.[63]

Never mind. Britain's government believes the earth is warming, believes that global warming creates dangerous possibilities

---

60 'Even now, the science of climate change remains provisional. However, BP Amoco believes that there is enough evidence to suggest that precautionary actions are prudent.' Michel de Fabiani (Regional President, Europe, BP Amoco), 'Business and Environmentalism', in Hogan and Stelzer, op. cit., p. 114.

61 For an interesting discussion of this and other points in the climate change debate, see Thomas C. Schelling, 'Costs & Benefits of Greenhouse Gas Reduction', *AEI Studies on Global Environmental Policy*, American Enterprise Institute, Washington, DC, 1998.

62 In this connection see Robert W. Hahn, *The Economics & Politics of Climate Change*, American Enterprise Institute, Washington, DC, 1998, pp. 25–36.

63 See reports in *The Times*, 20 February 2000. Some modelling predicts that global warming will benefit agricultural production in places such as the colder regions of Russia and Canada.

of floods, droughts and disease, and believes that the burning of fossil fuels is the culprit. It therefore says that it is determined to reduce the use of fossil fuels.[64]

In pursuit of such a reduction it has adopted several policies.

(i) The first is aimed at reducing the use of the automobile, which a study by the Royal Commission on Environmental Pollution alleges accounts for all of the projected increases in CO_2 emissions projected to occur through 2020. Steps taken include 'car-less days', modelled after the 'smokeless days' so beloved of the cigarette police the world over; bus lanes, which so far have had the disastrous effect of causing six-mile tailbacks on the road to Heathrow airport and, worse, trapping the Prime Minister's motorcade in one of the jams, forcing his ministerial car to use the bus lane for 'security reasons'; higher taxes on larger motor vehicles; and, most important, retaining the Tory policy of raising taxes on petrol by more than the rate of inflation. But that latter policy may soon be up for review: the government admits that the fuel escalator worked well when oil was selling for $10–$12 per barrel, but may not be appropriate with oil at $30.

This so-called 'anti-car policy' has caused such a backlash among voters that it is now being reviewed, with a view towards including some component of road-building and pro-auto ingredients in the overall policy stew.

---

64 Under the Kyoto agreement, Britain is bound to reduce its output of greenhouse gases by 12.5 per cent of 1990 levels by 2010. The government has promised to do even more: cut its output of CO_2 by 20 per cent. To achieve such a cut by relying on prices alone, the government's advisory unit estimates that gas prices would have to double and electricity prices increase by 50 per cent. *The Economist*, 27 June 1998, p. 56.

(ii) The second policy aimed at reducing emissions is to impose an energy tax, which the government prefers to call a 'climate change levy'.[65] This has led to several problems:

1. It has probably – the data are not entirely clear – shortened the effective economic life of the Bradwell nuclear plant.[66] Why energy produced in a nuclear plant should be subject to a climate change levy is clear only to government ministers, and adds to the suspicion that this tax is aimed at revenues for the Treasury as much as it is at cooling the globe.

2. Since the tax is on energy use, rather than on the carbon content of the fuels used to generate electricity, it only indirectly affects carbon dioxide emissions.

3. The tax bears so heavily on some companies that ministers will be empowered to grant tax relief if the company satisfies them that it is investing sufficiently in conservation. Naturally, the largest energy users will be in line for the greatest relief, hardly consistent with inducing cutbacks. And the scope for politically induced deals is considerable.

(iii) The third piece of the British government's energy/environmental policy is to increase spending (i.e. taxpayer investment) on mass transit, and to seek to lure private capital into that industry, so as to provide a better alternative to the use of the private automobile.

---

65   The cynical might argue that the goal of the higher taxes is more revenue for the Treasury.

66   See Ian Fells, Professor of Energy Conservation, University of Newcastle, in *The Times*, 7 January 2000.

(iv) The fourth part of the programme to reduce fossil fuel use is continuation of the Thatcher levy on electric users, with the funds used to subsidise non-fossil-fuel sources of energy. The great bulk of these funds has gone to the nuclear industry, which to everyone's surprise has markedly increased its efficiency and raised its market share from around 20 per cent to 25 per cent. Labour is eager to have more of these funds directed to wind farms and other renewables, on the ground that the cost of wind technology is coming down. Why it then needs a greater subsidy is unclear; and the government will undoubtedly face mounting complaints about the unsightliness of these machines in a country that has great affection for its green and pleasant landscape.

(v) The fifth strand of New Labour environmental policy is to throw its support behind efforts to convert the Kyoto protocol into real, live policy. The government is well aware of the American position that the cost of reducing greenhouse gasses will be markedly reduced in America if an international system for trading permits is instituted. And, like the rest of us, it is watching with interest the results of the internal permit trading system that BP has set up.[67] Indeed, New Labour says that it wants to do all it can to reduce the compliance costs to America, and indeed to other countries, by backing our efforts to have the other Kyoto signatories accede to our demand that an international permit trading system be established. The good news is that there are signs that the European Commission is moving

---

67   The company plans to reduce its emissions of greenhouse gases by 10 per cent of their 1990 levels by 2010.

towards accepting the necessity of some form of permit trading scheme.*

Summary

How might the government extricate itself from this mélange of contradictory policies? It could start by adopting the goal outlined in this paper: get the prices of various energy products right, and let competition handle the problem from then on. To get the prices right it must make certain that the externalities associated with the use of energy are internalised and reflected in prices, which would probably result in lowering petrol taxes while at the same time levying other user charges[68] on the automobile, and raising them on coal. It must also end its artificial interference with competition and, as Ofgem has suggested, allow gas to replace coal in the generation of electricity. The social costs associated with the displacement of miners should, like other externalities, be reflected in the price of gas, perhaps by the imposition of a tax on gas use sufficient to finance the retraining or retirement in dignity of the miners.

---

* The better news is that President Bush, knowing that the Senate would never approve the Kyoto protocol, has abandoned it, and is searching for a more sensible alternative, one not aimed at crippling American industry while leaving unaffected the developing countries who will account for most of the growth in greenhouse gas emissions.

68 See a sensible summary of the case for road charges and peak load pricing by Martin Wolf, *Financial Times*, 29 November 1999.

Soaring energy prices: market forces or market failure?

This talk was delivered at a conference sponsored by the Energy Daily *at the Watergate Hotel in Washington, DC, on 30 November 2000. Its primary goal was to lay out some policies that might restore competition to various energy markets, most notably the cartelised world market for crude oil. But the opportunity to comment on the energy fiasco in California proved irresistible.*

I have been asked to talk to you about what our hosts call 'soaring energy prices'. I can do that briefly – demand is rising, supply is not, so prices are going up. I would be delighted to take any questions. Thank you for your attention . . .

More seriously . . .

It seems to me that the best way to consider the question of whether the energy price situation we now confront – an increase in the level and the volatility of prices of electricity and oil (I leave the question of natural gas to others) – is a result of what we might reasonably call market forces, or of policy errors, is to take two examples: the market for electricity in California, and the market for oil and its products.

The advantage of juxtaposing these events is that it permits us to study one that, although of intense interest to its participants, is neither of fundamental importance nor difficult of solution, and one that is indeed of major importance and difficult in the extreme to solve.

The easier problem exists in California, where soaring spot prices for electricity upset consumers, and therefore the politicians who represent them. By saying that the problem is easier than the one we face in oil markets I do not mean to minimise the pain consumers feel in their wallets, the pain the utilities in the states are feeling on their income statements, or the pain politicians feel as they see anger in the eyes of their constituents.

What I *do* mean is that the problem can be designated as a minor one in three senses:

1. Rising and volatile electricity prices in California, although they have ripple effects and come at the inconvenient time of an economic slowdown, pose no threat to the existence of the nation, as do developments in the oil markets, to which I will turn in a moment. These price movements mainly concern questions of the distribution of income between the producers and the consumers of electricity. Such a distributional question, although of intense interest to the contestants for the income in question, is of less concern to economists, in part because they have less to contribute to such a debate than do, say, clergymen, ethicists, politicians and regulators.

Which is not to say that the battle over income distribution is of no consequence. When, as a very young economist, I told a regulator who sought my guidance in deciding how much of a utility's costs he should load onto residential as opposed to industrial customers 'That is merely a question of income distribution', he growled at me in response, 'So was the French Revolution.'

Still, I would argue that from a public policy point of view the question of whether consumers or producers of electricity should benefit from short-term shifts in the balance of supply and demand need not detain us for long.

2. The second sense in which the California situation is of less fundamental policy importance than it might seem from the headlines it is attracting is that there is a less complex problem than meets the eye. I think it not unfair to say that the architects of the

California system that replaced the traditional regulatory regime designed a Rube Goldberg contraption that had not the slightest chance of functioning anything like a workably competitive market, which relies on price as a tool to balance demand and supply. These architects began by accepting a situation in which most consumers remain ignorant of what they are paying for the electricity they are currently consuming; they erected effective barriers to new entrants; they prevented free dealing by sellers and buyers, requiring them instead to filter their offers through a Soviet-style central agency; they prevented participants from hedging or from negotiating long-term contracts; they prevented the construction of new capacity; and their fellow policy-makers imposed on one important supplier the obligation to elevate the welfare of young salmon in the North over the welfare of aged consumers in the South. Having finished designing this wondrous machine the policy gurus now profess surprise that a system thus constructed produces peculiar results!

I recognise, of course, that this is a bit of an oversimplification, although I would be interested to learn from this expert audience which of these points is not correct. But I think it not unreasonable to argue that, having sown the wind, policy-makers in California cannot be surprised that they are inheriting the windmill, rather than some more economic source of much-needed generating capacity!

Indeed, it is not at all clear to me that the situation in California is not the one that Californians themselves prefer. After all, the citizens of the state were just given a choice between a presidential candidate [George W. Bush] who favours increasing the supply of energy, and one [Al Gore] who has spent his career opposing any such increases. They overwhelmingly chose the latter. Even if we move all the votes by Californians who have dimples into the Bush column, we would not have close to a majority in favour of the candidate who calls for increasing energy supplies.

3. A final reason why it is fair to consider the California situation less than terribly serious is that it is on its way to solution, or, more precisely, that the contours of a solution are visible to all who would see. Never mind that, noticing that there is a shortage, the politicians and born-again regulators have decided to cure it by putting a cap on prices – a technique learned from New York City's rent controllers and now-unemployed crafters of Gosplan. Some of the state's legislators have suggested to me that an equally efficacious solution would be to ban the export of electricity from the state – a sort of reverse mercantilism. Judging by the availability of academics to defend the notion that a majority of the popular vote in the recent election has constitutional meaning, I am sure at least one constitutional scholar can be found on some California campus to defend such an export ban.

All of that said, there is one sense in which developments in California can be deemed to be of real significance. If policy-makers see in the flawed efforts of the state to replace regulation with competitive markets a warning to go slow on deregulation, the nation may pay a price that it need not. The California experiment failed because those who concocted the system now in operation did not trust free markets to produce efficient pricing and optimal utilisation of the state's energy resources. To question the superiority of markets over regulation on the basis of the California experience would be tantamount to rejecting free-market capitalism because the Russian version of capitalism has so far proved shambolic.

So I will spend no more time this morning on the California situation. As I said, the problem can and will be solved, for several reasons: the nature of the problem and its proximate causes are clear; some of the best minds in the academic and consulting world, including Alfred Kahn, Harvard's Bill Hogan and MIT's Paul Joskow, have turned their attention to this problem; the utilities have an enormous stake in coming up with a solution that both protects them from immediate short-term financial disaster and the longer-term, enduring wrath of their customers; the regulators and politicians cannot seriously contemplate penalising the utilities unless they find evidence of market manipulation; the politicians I have met now have the benefit of experience with the flawed system, and several have said quite sensible things about possible solutions. They have told me that they must devise some way to allow utilities to enter into long-term contracts and hedging arrangements without fear that regulators will second-guess them if spot markets prove to be soft, and they seem to recognise that the future welfare of their constituents requires easier entry for new competitors.[*]

Most important, the choices before the state's citizens and policy-makers as they attempt to balance environmental considerations against the need for more electricity are now clearer. No one can any longer promise a free lunch – no new plants but lots of cheap energy. The 'new economy' industries that have brought prosperity to the state are proving surprisingly (to some) as energy-intensive as the old economy's refineries and steel mills. Californians now must make some hard choices, and live with the

---

[*]   In the event, my faith in the rationality of politicians proved misplaced. Price caps remain at the retail level; one utility has declared bankruptcy; and the state has taken over the chore of purchasing power at wholesale and of operating the transmission system, in the process squandering its budget surplus.

consequences. If they avoid the difficult cost-benefit analysis that must be done, if they think that price caps can somehow end shortages, if they believe that environmental considerations are absolute, rather than merely one factor to be included in a complicated decision-making process – then their problem should not command too much of our attention and sympathy. We should not expend valuable intellectual resources attempting to heal self-inflicted wounds.

Let me turn now to the second case we have before us of rising prices – oil markets. I would argue that the problem we as a nation face in oil markets dwarfs in importance the problem faced in California, for several reasons:

- The subversion of free markets by a cartel affects not merely the distribution of income between various segments of American society, as is broadly the case in California; it affects as well the distribution of income between consumers here and worldwide, on the one hand, and the regimes of the oil-producing nations.
- Whereas shortages of electricity in California merely (and I use that word without meaning to be insensitive to local economic problems) have some unpleasant consequences for that state's economy, and for those feeling its ripple effects, the ability of a cartel to create shortages of oil gives it the ability to abort the nation's long-term economic growth and to tip the economy into recession.
- Whereas problems of electricity supply in California may create some tensions between state and federal authorities, problems of oil supply create tensions between nations. The tensions in California can be settled in a hearing room; those in oil markets

have been and may again be settled on the battlefield.

Perhaps most important, the problems we face in oil markets seriously affect our ability to conduct an independent foreign policy. This is not only because the present administration [at the time of this talk, the Clinton administration] instinctively chooses grovelling as an instrument of foreign policy, allowing its Secretary of State to be treated with discourtesy bordering on contempt by Syria, which does not even have any oil to offer. It is because any administration cannot help feeling the burden of our economic dependence on undemocratic, volatile nations in the Middle East and, lately, in Latin America when attempting to forge a foreign policy that reflects America's interests.

In short, just as in California, we face in oil markets the consequences of impediments to the functioning of free markets. In California, those impediments are now obvious, and the solutions are heaving into view, to borrow a phrase from my nautical friends. (At least, I hope I have the phrase right; sailing is not one of the arts practised in my old neighbourhood, since the open fire hydrants were not capable of creating bodies of water deep enough to accommodate the vessels I see going to and fro on Chesapeake Bay.) In the case of oil, the source of the problem is obvious, but the solution remains elusive.

In the remaining few minutes, let me lay out the problem, and review with you some possible solutions.

The problem is that a long-standing cartel has found new cohesion, and is restricting supply so as to keep the price of crude oil at many multiples of the marginal cost of new production – somewhere between three and ten times that cost, depending on which estimate of what it costs to find, develop and produce new reserves in the Middle East you choose to credit. The OPEC cartel's task has been made easier by a series of events:

- The long period of economic growth in America came to coincide with a modest recovery in the economies of Europe and resumed economic growth in Asia, pushing up the demand for oil at unexpected rates.
- Embargoes of oil from three large producing nations – Iran, Libya and Iraq – have reduced (although not eliminated) supplies flowing from those countries onto world markets.
- The fright and financial pressures unleashed in producing countries by $10 oil brought the Middle Eastern and other producing nations together as no mere appeals to unity could ever do.
- Mexico decided that it could persuade Saudi Arabia and Venezuela to cut back production by promising not to fill the supply gap that such cutbacks would create in the United States. Mexico, a non-member, in effect joined OPEC.
- The Venezuelan government came under the control of an anti-American radical, determined to change the distribution of the world's income in favour of developing nations, and to tweak the nose of Uncle Sam by falling in line with Fidel Castro's hemispheric policy goals.
- American policy-makers, in pursuit of environmental objectives, decided not to develop the nation's own oil and gas resources to their fullest, to make it somewhere between difficult and impossible to build new oil-processing facilities, and to make the use of coal increasingly difficult.*

---

* The Bush administration is attempting to reverse these policies.

- Environmentalists would add still another cause of our current discomfort: failure to adopt policies that discourage the use of oil, including further restrictions on the safe and comfortable SUVs that the Vice-President [Al Gore] uses to transport himself from his residence to meetings with his EPA administrator to plot methods for forcing others into smaller, less safe and less comfortable vehicles.

What is to be done?

One possibility that must be considered seriously is to do nothing. After all, cartels have a history of collapsing when members begin to cheat on their quotas, or when the artificially high prices set by the cartelists attract non-members into the industry, augmenting supply and producing a price collapse. Both cheating and new entry have characterised the oil industry in the past, so why not apply the famous dictum, attributed to Ronald Reagan, 'Don't do something, just stand there', a policy that often served the nation well during President Reagan's terms in office.

I fear that in this case inaction is not a real option. The new-found cohesiveness of OPEC, and the rapacity it has recently exhibited, create two problems for such a passive strategy.

- While waiting for the cartel to collapse, American consumers will pay a very substantial annual toll, and suffer the macroeconomic consequences induced by the payment of such a 'tax' – slower growth and higher inflation being the most notable.
- Waiting for the development of non-OPEC sources and alternatives to oil may prove as productive as waiting for

Godot. Although there remain substantial undiscovered reserves of oil in non-OPEC areas, it is not safe to rely on new entrants to drive down prices in an industry in which incumbent cartelists sit on vast quantities of non-producing, low-cost reserves. Potential newcomers to the oil game and those who finance them, and existing players who have to decide on their exploration budgets, are well aware that, should their exploration activities threaten the cartel, it can open its valves and make the new entrants' projects uneconomic. That doesn't mean that drillers are completely insensitive to the lure created by higher prices, but it does suggest that they respond more slowly and less completely to oil price run-ups than they would if the threat of OPEC predation did not loom over their spreadsheets.

So, too, with developers of alternatives to oil-using technologies. These entrepreneurs have long complained that they find it difficult to get financial backing because potential investors know that the Saudis and their cartel colleagues can at any time force oil prices down and make promising alternative technologies uneconomic. Which is one reason, when prices soared above $30, why the Saudis began very publicly contemplating increasing output sufficiently to bring prices down to around $25. The Saudis, with almost 100 years of proved reserves and more to be found with little effort, are in the business for the long pull, and will do what it takes to discourage investors in new technologies from seizing their markets. Although the development of alternatives to oil as an automotive fuel is likely to continue, other technologies face an uphill battle in the face of OPEC's ability to pick price points that can change the economics of these alternatives from attractive to dismal.

These hard facts suggest that passivity is not an appropriate energy policy for America: the supply responses that would occur in a free market faced with shortages and soaring prices are subject to attenuation by a powerful cartel.

Another possibility is to rely on the Strategic Petroleum Reserve as a counter to OPEC. That, too, seems to me a non-starter. History suggests that there are two reasons to believe that efforts to use the SPR to keep prices closer to competitive levels will not work.

The first is that the private sector will reduce its own inventories in parallel with the government's increase in the SPR. Private companies hold inventories for a variety of reasons: to protect long-term customers in the event of a supply interruption; to assure the steady operation of capital-intensive facilities such as refineries; to profit from price spikes that might emerge in temporary periods of increased demand. But if the government stands ready to perform that function, the incentive to incur the costs of carrying inventory is reduced. Which seems to have been the case in oil-consuming countries, according to a Harvard University study:

> ... While the size of strategic stockpiles has grown in the United States, Japan, and some Western European countries, the size of private stocks has fallen significantly. The net effect has been that the total size of the industrial countries' oil stockpiles was smaller in 1987 than at the start of the decade. Indeed, the growth of strategic stockpiles may have contributed to the drawdown of commercial inventories.[69]

69 Bijan Mossavar-Rahmani, William H. Hogan, Dale W. Jorgenson and Richard N. Cooper, 'Lower Oil Prices: Mapping the Impact', Harvard University Energy and Environmental Policy Center, 1988, pp. 4–5.

A second reason for being wary of relying on government use of a strategic reserve as an effective policy tool is quite simply the history of the SPR. We have pumped into storage some 570 million barrels, but have never quite figured out how to use it. Recently, we released a few barrels from the reserve only to find that the government does not know how to conduct an auction – some of the bidders proved less than financially viable – and that OPEC could credibly threaten to reduce its output barrel for barrel to match the draw-down of the SPR. Alternatively, our policymakers, from the President on down to officials at the Department of Energy, have held that the reserve is to be used only when the last drop of available oil has been consumed – when the storage tanks are empty, the gasoline stations closed, and unfortunate residents of the Northeast reduced to firewood and sweaters to protect themselves from the miserable winter. Even during one of the largest military build-ups in the history of the world – our massing of forces to drive Saddam out of Kuwait – when oil prices doubled, the reserve remained untouched, the Bush-the-elder administration holding to the view that a war in the largest oil-producing region of the world, and a consequent doubling of oil prices, did not constitute an emergency.

If doing nothing is too costly to be a viable policy, and if relying on the SPR would represent the triumph of hope over experience, what can be done? We can fashion a policy that is aimed at making oil markets work better – not as a perfectly competitive market would operate, but at least as an effectively competitive one would.

On the demand side, that means making the prices that signal consumers, who must choose between use and abstinence, correctly reflect all of the costs (private and social) associated with a decision in favour of use. On the supply side, a market-oriented energy policy must seek to eliminate or, if that is impossible, counteract artificial constraints on the ability of supply to respond to price signals.

Let's first consider what we might do to enhance supply.

We might begin by re-examining the cost-benefit analyses that have led us to make oil storage more expensive (with a consequent reduction in vendors' willingness to maintain inventories), and to restrict domestic exploration and production. It might have made sense to ban offshore drilling and Arctic exploration when oil was selling for $10 per barrel. But the calculus that led us to restrict domestic supplies of oil at that price may not hold when potential output is valued at three times that level. Although calculations showing that the environmental costs of opening now-restricted areas are exceeded by the benefits of increased domestic production are unlikely to persuade the greenest of our greens that the national interest dictates a change in policy,[70] anything other than a Gore-dominated EPA might well find such arithmetic persuasive, especially since the Department of Energy has recently trebled its mean estimate of recoverable oil reserves along the coast of Alaska's national wildlife refuge to 10.3 billion barrels, which would represent an addition of at least one-third to America's oil reserves.[71]

The next step to enhance supply would be to mount a multifaceted and credible attack on OPEC's supply constraints. This would begin by recognising that Mexico is a key player in the

---

70 Commenting on increased estimates of the volume and value of recoverable reserves in the closed Arctic areas, Melinda Price, senior Washington lobbyist for the Sierra Club, said, 'No amount of oil is worth sacrificing this spectacular landscape and its value to Americans.' *Wall Street Journal*, 24 May 2000.

71 Ibid.

recent trebling of oil prices, and taking steps to persuade our southern neighbour that such behaviour is not in its long-term interest. Although not a member of OPEC, Mexico brokered the deal between Venezuela and Saudi Arabia that eventuated in the sharp cutback in output that triggered the price rise, and cleared the way for OPEC's agreement to close its valves by promising not to step up its own sales to the United States.

Query: Why is the American government, which bailed out the Mexican economy when the peso collapsed and has bestowed the benefits of NAFTA on Mexico, reluctant to read the Riot Act to the Mexican government? True, the benefits of NAFTA are not Mexico's alone. American consumers are also beneficiaries of the increased improvement in the international division of labour. But sometimes policy trade-offs must be made, and it would seem that the first step in an effective energy policy, one that aims to bring the price of oil closer to the level that would prevail in a free market, might well be to explain to the Mexicans that they cannot hope to sell the output of their *maquiladoras* and their T-shirts, trainers and automobiles to us unless they also offer us oil at competitive prices.

The lost benefit of low-cost Mexican consumer goods would surely be more than offset by the lower oil prices that would result from such a demonstration of our willingness to use our massive purchasing power to persuade the new government of Mexico that it is not in its long-term interests to facilitate and participate in the exploitation of the American consumer.

A similar effort to induce an increase in supplies might be applied to Kuwait, a nation on which Saddam Hussein still has designs. Kuwait possesses about 10 per cent of the world's proved reserves of oil, but accounts for only some 3 per cent of world output. It is one of the OPEC members with large amounts of spare production capacity, giving it the ability to turn on its taps at short notice. Put another way, the country that we saved from destruction, while its ruling family waited out the war in London's Dorchester Hotel and in Harrods, could continue to produce at current levels for well over 100 years without discovering another barrel of oil. We might even consider establishing a policy that relates our contribution to Kuwait's defence to the level of oil output set by the Kuwaiti royal family!

Again, we face a trade-off. If we threaten to abandon the Kuwaitis to their fate unless they step up production, we are threatening ourselves with the loss of the country's oil and the aggrandisement of the Iraqi despot. But the consequences to us would be some inconvenience; the consequences to the Kuwaitis would be annihilation. Guess who would blink first.

Another plank of any sensible supply-enhancing energy policy would involve a review of our sanctions programme. Libya, Iran and Iraq between them account for almost one-quarter of the world's oil reserves (approximately 3 per cent, 10 per cent and 10 per cent, respectively). Our reasons for pressing our balky allies to continue the embargo against Iraq remain as strong, or stronger, than ever, although the embargo is increasingly porous and under continuing threat from the French, who boast that they have never allowed questions of morality, or notions of gratitude and loyalty to allies, to interfere with their commercial interests.

But a relaxation of the embargo of Iran might – just might – prove justified if a deal could be struck with that increasingly hard-pressed country. After years of underfunding, Iran's oil industry is badly in need of investment if it is even to maintain its production capacity at current levels. It is in our interest as well as Iran's for that country to increase its proved reserves and its capacity to produce those reserves – but only if Iran agrees, in return for the lifting of the ban on American oil company investment, to step up output sufficiently to bring world oil prices closer to the marginal cost of exploration, development and production.

Then there are our antitrust laws, statutes from which the Arab and other oil producers have been uniquely exempt for political reasons. That the laws could be used to prosecute the cartelists there is little doubt. After all, the Department of Justice has successfully brought actions against German, Japanese and French cartels in products as diverse as citric acid, lysine, vitamins and fax paper. In most of these cases the cartelists had no offices in America; they merely sold products here. Indeed, in the case of fax paper, the 1st Circuit Court of Appeals has upheld the Antitrust Division's suit against Nippon Paper, a company that did not sell directly to the United States, but fixed the prices of those who did.

It is of course the case, as my lawyer friends point out, that American law grants foreign sovereigns immunity from antitrust prosecution, and grants similar immunity to companies acting under the compulsion of foreign sovereigns. But that law is no real barrier to prosecution if there is a will to move against OPEC. For one thing, the so-called 'commercial activity exemption' allows the Antitrust Division to proceed if it decides that the sovereign governments are engaged merely in commercial activity, like selling oil, which the OPEC members contend, presumably with straight faces, is much more than mere commercial activity – it is, they say, the preservation of their national patrimony. For another, laws can be repealed or amended: this exemption can always be removed.

Such a move would permit the antitrust authorities to take action against the Saudis and other producing countries, all of which have substantial assets in America, assets that could be attached to satisfy any legitimate claims against those governments and the companies co-operating with them to maintain oil prices at anti-competitive levels. But it seems that a variety of political considerations (most notably pressure from the Arabists in the State Department) have stayed the Antitrust Division's hand by preventing it from using the commercial activity exemption or obtaining the necessary legislation from Congress – although what the State Department's diplomats have obtained from countries that persist in conspiring to elevate the level of world oil prices is difficult to discern.

Finally, we must consider the demand side of the oil supply equation. The fact that the goals of some of the groups that would curtail the use of oil have more to do with a Luddite desire to turn back the clock of industrialisation than with meeting the problem of our dependence on unstable supply sources should not deter us from exploring the demand side.

The first step is to make certain that the prices consumers are paying for oil products reflect the marginal cost they are imposing on society by virtue of their consumption. Measures might include increased taxes on oil use to reflect any uninternalised costs of oil use, with the proceeds used to reduce marginal income tax rates and other initiative-stifling taxes. If it is indeed the case that oil embargoes or cartel-induced price run-ups can threaten us with dire macroeconomic consequences, including rising unemployment, then the cost of such economy-wide upheavals should be reflected in the price of oil products, so that consumers of gasoline and other petroleum products bear the full costs they impose on society by their consumption.

Richard Berner, chief US economist at Morgan Stanley Dean Witter, estimates that every $5 increase in the price of a barrel of oil knocks 0.3 percentage points off our GDP over a year.[72] That suggests that the recent run-up can cost our economy something like a full percentage point of GDP. And perhaps add one percentage point to the inflation rate, according to Mark Zandi, of Regional Financial Associates.[73] This may not be a problem at a time when the economy is booming, but in the less pleasant economic circumstances that many predict await us in the new year [2001], the loss of that much GDP will have quite noticeable consequences.

Besides, if we choose higher oil prices as the means of slowing an overheating economy, it would be far wiser to raise taxes on oil (and, I repeat, keep those funds from spendthrift Washington politicians by reducing other taxes in parallel) rather than to allow OPEC to do the equivalent by raising prices. Better for the money to flow to our Treasury for recycling than to have it finance the construction of still more Middle Eastern palaces, or the operation of terrorist groups, or be spent in a doomed effort to maintain political stability by continuing to fund the extremely generous 'social contract' that the Saudi rulers agreed with their subjects when oil revenues were high.

We can also take action on the demand side by determining whether demand-side measures that were uneconomic when oil was at $10 per barrel are worth pursuing when prices are two or three times that level. Many may well be.

Keep in mind, however, that if we get the prices of oil and its

---

72　*Financial Times*, 20 July 2000.
73　*International Herald Tribune*, 24 February 2000.

products right – at competitive levels, and including all costs associated with their use – there is little scope for government action on the demand side except to make such minor, as yet unattained improvements in the flow of information to consumers as might be cost-effective.

It should be emphasised that none of the components of the market-oriented energy policy I have described involves government control of prices, or subsidies to producers of oil or alternative technologies. Such policies have failed in the past, and are certain to fail in the future. But a programme to introduce more competition by weakening the cartel through diplomatic pressure and antitrust actions; to enhance supply by explaining to those dependent on the American military umbrella to shield them from a rain of missiles and to those who rely on our export markets for their prosperity that we expect reciprocal decency; and to adjust environmental and tax policies to the new reality of the increased cohesiveness of OPEC members, is one that will make energy markets work better, increasing the strength of Adam Smith's invisible hand without inviting into the daily marketplace the long arm of government.

In short: America has the diplomatic, economic and legal weapons with which to blast the cartel; it has so far chosen to leave them in their holsters.

ABOUT THE IEA

The Institute is a research and educational charity (No. CC 235 351), limited by guarantee. Its mission is to improve understanding of the fundamental institutions of a free society with particular reference to the role of markets in solving economic and social problems.

The IEA achieves its mission by:

- a high-quality publishing programme
- conferences, seminars, lectures and other events
- outreach to school and college students
- brokering media introductions and appearances

The IEA, which was established in 1955 by the late Sir Antony Fisher, is an educational charity, not a political organisation. It is independent of any political party or group and does not carry on activities intended to affect support for any political party or candidate in any election or referendum, or at any other time. It is financed by sales of publications, conference fees and voluntary donations.

In addition to its main series of publications the IEA also publishes a quarterly journal, *Economic Affairs*, and has two specialist programmes – Environment and Technology, and Education.

The IEA is aided in its work by a distinguished international Academic Advisory Council and an eminent panel of Honorary Fellows. Together with other academics, they review prospective IEA publications, their comments being passed on anonymously to authors. All IEA papers are therefore subject to the same rigorous independent refereeing process as used by leading academic journals.

IEA publications enjoy widespread classroom use and course adoptions in schools and universities. They are also sold throughout the world and often translated/reprinted.

Since 1974 the IEA has helped to create a world-wide network of 100 similar institutions in over 70 countries. They are all independent but share the IEA's mission.

Views expressed in the IEA's publications are those of the authors, not those of the Institute (which has no corporate view), its Managing Trustees, Academic Advisory Council members or senior staff.

Members of the Institute's Academic Advisory Council, Honorary Fellows, Trustees and Staff are listed on the following page.

The Institute gratefully acknowledges financial support for its publications programme and other work from a generous benefaction by the late Alec and Beryl Warren.

235

For information about subscriptions to IEA publications, please contact:

Subscriptions
The Institute of Economic Affairs
2 Lord North Street
London SW1P 3LB

Tel: 020 7799 8900
Fax: 020 7799 2137
Website: www.iea.org.uk/books/subscribe.htm

Other papers recently published by the IEA include:

WHO, What and Why?

Transnational Government, Legitimacy and the World Health Organization
Roger Scruton
Occasional Paper 113
ISBN 0 255 36487 3

The World Turned Rightside Up

A New Trading Agenda for the Age of Globalisation
John C. Hulsman
Occasional Paper 114
ISBN 0 255 36495 4

The Representation of Business in English Literature

Introduced and edited by Arthur Pollard
Readings 53
ISBN 0 255 36491 1

Anti-Liberalism 2000

The Rise of New Millennium Collectivism
David Henderson
Occasional Paper 115
ISBN 0 255 36497 0

Capitalism, Morality and Markets
Brian Griffiths, Robert A. Sirico, Norman Barry & Frank Field
Readings 54
ISBN 0 255 36496 2

A Conversation with Harris and Seldon
Ralph Harris & Arthur Seldon
Occasional Paper 116
ISBN 0 255 36498 9

Malaria and the DDT Story
Richard Tren & Roger Bate
Occasional Paper 117
ISBN 0 255 36499 7

A Plea to Economists Who Favour Liberty: Assist the Everyman
Daniel B. Klein
Occasional Paper 118
ISBN 0 255 36501 2

Waging the War of Ideas
John Blundell
Occasional Paper 119
ISBN 0 255 36500 4